Making Progress

EDUCATION AND CULTURE
IN NEW TIMES

Making Progress

EDUCATION AND CULTURE
IN NEW TIMES

Dennis Carlson

Teachers College, Columbia University
New York and London

Published by Teachers College Press, 1234 Amsterdam Avenue, New York, NY 10027

Library of Congress Cataloging-in-Publication Data

Carlson, Dennis.
  Making progress : education and culture in new times / Dennis
Carlson.
     p.   cm.
  Includes bibliographical references and index.
    ISBN 0-8077-3577-9 (alk. paper). — ISBN 0-8077-3576-0 (pbk. :
alk. paper)
    1. Multicultural education—United States. 2. Educational
anthropology—United States. 3. Educational change—United States.
I. Title.
LC1099.3.C373 1997
370.19′6′0973—dc20   96-28695

ISBN 0-8077-3576-0 (paper)
ISBN 0-8077-3577-9 (cloth)

Printed on acid-free paper
Manufactured in the United States of America

04   03   02   01   00   99   98   97   8   7   6   5   4   3   2   1

Contents

v

Acknowledgments

ONE OF THE MOST effective ways to "make progress" in democratic societies, as in our lives I believe, is to stay open to possibilities that present themselves to us. Rather than construct grand plans in which every step is neatly predetermined and the outcome is clear and fixed, it is best to take one step at a time. So this book has come to be written. It had its beginnings in long dinner and lunch conversations over several years with Brian Ellerbeck at Teachers College Press. He encouraged me in my thoughts about a book, helped me clarify ideas, and was always supportive. The first essay I wrote for this book, on sexuality education, was written originally at the request of my friend and colleague, Jim Sears, for inclusion in a book he was editing on *Sexuality and the Curriculum* that subsequently was published by Teachers College Press. The idea for the essay emerged over a long walk and dialogue as we viewed the AIDS Project Quilt in Washington, DC in the summer of 1989. I often think that without Jim's prodding, this essay would not be. The next essay to be drafted was Chapter 4 on multicultural education, although it has gone through many redrafts since then and been presented at several conferences in one version or another before being published in *Curriculum Inquiry*. Of those whose ideas have helped me in writing this chapter, I want to thank Cameron McCarthy in particular. His work always challenges me to see the complexity of the struggle over multicultural education. I also want to thank Michael Apple for his input and for allowing me the opportunity to present an early draft of this essay to his Friday seminar of doctoral students at the University of Wisconsin–Madison. Thomas Oldenski encouraged me to publish this essay in journal form and helped me assess the contributions of critical pedagogy. Finally, Julia Carlson (who just happens to be my mother and an intellectual in her own right) took a keen interest in this essay and made many useful suggestions for revisions. Chapter 2 also has gone through many revisions and drafts as a conference paper before being published in revised form in *Educational Theory*. Aside from several anonymous reviewers who provided comments, I want to thank Nicholas Burbules, editor of *Educational Theory*, for his time and effort in helping me frame this essay. My former colleagues at the Miami University Center for Education and Cultural Studies, Henry Giroux and Peter McLaren, along with David Trend, contributed in important ways to my analysis of postmodern theory in

this chapter. Chapters 6 and 7 were written over the past several years. I want
to thank Michelle Fine and Lois Weis for encouraging me to write both essays
and for their editorial advice in revising them. William Pink encouraged me
to submit Chapter 6 on "gayness" and multicultural education to the journal
Educational Foundations, where it first was published. Chapter 7, on coloni-
ial and postcolonial education, has been much influenced by Sandra Cole-
McNaught, who has helped me understand the growing literature on postcolonialism. Chapter 3, on tracking and detracking, was the next chapter to be
written and appears for the first time in print in this book. Especially influential
in helping shape my thoughts for this essay was Like Lokon, a graduate assistant
at Miami University who has been working with me on a study of a "detracked"
school-within-a-school in a nearby urban school district. In our drives back and
forth to the school, we talked about the challenge of "detracking" schools in
a tracked society. The first chapter, on the ideas of progress and progressivism,
was written last. I want to thank Jim Garrison and Richard Quantz for helping
me assess Deweyan pragmatism; Kathleen Knight, Peter Magolda, and Lori
Varlotti for helping me develop a critique of communitarianism; and Dan Reyes,
a doctoral assistant with the Center for Education and Cultural Studies at Miami
University, who explored various texts on progress in the twentieth century and
helped me contextualize progressivism in education. Lastly, I must thank Kent
Peterson for being there throughout the writing of this book.

Introduction

THE ESSAYS THAT make up this book have been written over the past 5 years, and most of them have been published in modified form as journal articles or chapters in edited books. Nevertheless, all of the chapters have been, from the beginning, part of a larger project on the forging of a democratic progressive educational policy and practice capable of responding to specific struggles going on over the direction of public education and American culture as we enter a new historical era. It is my belief that we are at one of those critical junctures in our history—an unsettling time in which established beliefs and practices are being questioned as never before, in which marginalized groups are no longer accepting their marginalized status, and in which calls by those on the political right to return order and discipline to society, and to roll back the gains made by workers, women, African Americans and Hispanics, gays and lesbians, and others, have a strong appeal. In such unsettling, "postmodern" times it is imperative, I believe, that those of us committed to a democratic, caring society be able to articulate a persuasive response. It is to this end that this book is dedicated. Each chapter critiques some aspect of existing practices in public schools, explores the limitations of current neoconservative and neoliberal reform movements in public education, and offers some suggestions in the way of formulating a democratic progressive response. The journey in each case is from a language of critique to a language of engagement and hope.

Chapter 1 examines the idea of progress as a modernist construct, inextricably interrelated with the belief that reason and the scientific method will lead us to the "good society." History, then, is the story of the gradual improvement of society in the direction of a utopian vision. Unfortunately, I argue, the idea of progress has not always or even primarily served democratic interests and values. Dominant strands of progressivism in education in this century have been grounded in economic and disciplinary visions of the good society, and these progressive discourses of reform continue to be most influential in shaping public education in the late twentieth century. I then examine the discourse and practice of democratic progressivism in this century, linking it to Deweyan pragmatism and social reconstructionism, and suggest how democratic progressive discourse is changing under the influence of postmodern theory.

Chapter 2 examines broad shifts occurring in postmodern society and explores their implications for the reinvention of public education. Specifically, I explore the contributions of three different strands of postmodern theory to the formulation of a democratic progressive discourse on educational renewal. The first of these is represented by theorists of the "new social movements," in which the emphasis is on an increasingly diverse culture organized around movements of lifestyle, identity, and values. A second group of theorists of "post-fordist" society, working out of a neo-Marxist tradition, focus our attention on the influence of economic restructuring in shaping the postmodern cultural and political landscape. Finally, Michel Foucault's (1979) work suggests shifts in contemporary culture toward the increasing individualization of surveillance and control, along with increasing resistance to the power of the state and professional "experts" to control our lives and define who we are.

Chapter 3 focuses on recent reform movements in public education associated with "detracking." Democratic progressives have long opposed ability-grouping practices and the separation of academic and vocational tracks in secondary education. Such tracking practices have been integral to the role public schools play in both producing and reproducing inequality. Yet, suddenly it seems that everyone, including elite business groups and state officials, is jumping on the detracking bandwagon. How can we account for such apparently democratic reforms in a conservative age? I suggest that beneath the veneer of detracking, the nation's schools are being retracked in ways that produce greater inequality rather than less. A serious effort to detrack the nation's schools, I argue, must challenge the role of schooling in social reproduction, along with taken-for-granted beliefs based on dualisms of "success/failure," "high ability/ low ability," "mental/manual," and so forth, that are implicated in tracking practices.

Multicultural education is the subject of Chapter 4. Like detracking, almost everyone supports some form of multicultural education these days. I interpret multicultural education as a "settlement" that emerged out of the civil rights struggles of the 1960s. As a settlement, I suggest that it has helped advance democratic projects in some ways but has been severely limited by the fact that it has been integrated, in schools, within a dominant discourse and practice that block its full potential. These limitations have to do with the incorporation of multicultural education as one more subject within a highly fragmented curriculum, the tendency to treat bias and prejudice as individual psychological phenomena, and the tendency to treat identity as natural and fixed rather than socially constructed and historically emergent. Multicultural education must be a central theme of any democratic progressive discourse designed to prepare young people for an increasingly diverse culture, but the limitations of current versions of multicultural education will need to be seriously addressed in doing so.

Chapter 5 examines the volatile and entrenched battle being waged over sexuality education in U.S. schools. I examine four cultural theories of sexuality that have had at least some limited influence over shaping the practice of sexuality education in the twentieth century, and I associate each with different interest groups and politics. These cultural theories of sexuality include a repressive theory that associates sexuality with sin and sickness; a utilitarian theory that has sought better methods of managing adolescent sexuality to reduce the social costs of unwanted pregnancies and venereal disease; a postconventional theory that explicitly links sexuality to culture and to power relations; and a libertarian theory that has understood sexuality in terms of meeting individual needs and negotiating sexual relations with others. Democratic progressivism, I argue, needs to blend elements of libertarianism, with its emphasis on individual rights, with elements of postconventional theory, with its emphasis on the cultural production of sexuality within power relations.

Chapter 6 examines the role public education has played, and continues to play, in the oppression and marginalization of gays and lesbians. This has involved the invisibility of "gayness" in the curriculum, the tacit sanctioning of verbal and physical harassment of gay students and teachers, and the "witch-hunting," silencing, and dismissal of gay and lesbian teachers. I suggest that while public schools continue to be heavily implicated in the reproduction of homophobia, this increasingly is being challenged by the new visibility of lesbians and gays in popular culture and by a new generation of young gay people and teachers who are demanding to be heard. I conclude this chapter with some reflections on the recent conflict over the so-called Rainbow Curriculum in New York City schools.

Chapter 7, unlike the others, includes personal narrative. One of the characteristics of postmodern scholarship is a return to narrative, story, and autobiography. In this case, I tell several stories from personal experience that are organized around a common theme: colonial and postcolonial education. Recent postcolonial scholars are making us aware of just how much the dominant, Eurocentric culture has, through the modern project of colonial expansionism, constructed an image of the colonial Other as developmentally retarded, culturally and intellectually deficient, lazy, irresponsible, and subservient. The two stories I tell are of working and observing in schools that were heavily influenced by colonial beliefs and practices. The first story is about working in a Navajo reservation boarding school as part of Peace Corps training in the late 1960s; the second is about my recent work in an inner-city school serving poor African American and Appalachian students. Although these are primarily stories of education that disempowers more than it empowers, I also suggest that in both schools an incipient postcolonial discourse and practice were to be found.

1

Progress, Progressivism, and Postmodernism in Education

IN MY UNIVERSITY classes for teachers pursuing a master's degree and for undergraduate students about to enter the profession of teaching, I often have found one "text" particularly useful in helping to begin a discussion of progressivism in American education. It is an editorial printed in the *National Education Association Journal* in the early 1920s under the title "Earth's Noblest Monument" (1923). Actually, much of this text consists of a large editorial graphic: a huge building of the modern skyscraper type dominates the foreground and is labeled "schools." In the background and to the left are two much smaller but clearly related architectural signifiers: the U.S. Capitol and the Washington Monument, serving to link public schools with the ideals of democracy. To the right and in the background is a snow-capped mountain and a tall fir tree, representing the wonders of the natural world, which pale in comparison to the school. The text below the graphic begins with the assertion that progress is being made at a rapid rate in modern society so that, for example, where once there were more prisons than libraries, "now there are more libraries than prisons." Nevertheless, if the public library is a monument to democratic culture, according to the text,

> there is one monument that dwarfs all others, making them seem insignificant. The noblest of monuments is the public school . . . The public school is DEMOCRATIC. It receives and treats all alike: wealth does not count, poverty does not hinder. The knowledge and the books are there for ALL. . . . It [public education] teaches THE FACTS that all intelligent human beings accept. . . . The public school recognizes only social equality. The HEAD of the class is for the child that studies, and the bottom of the class for the child that does not study. The only aristocracy is that of learning, of application, of good conduct. . . . The public school is the United States in miniature. In it the little citizens that are to be the future voters sit side by side, all Equal. (p. 115)

The essay acknowleges that public schools still have progress to make in some areas. For example, "the teachers are not paid yet as they should be, but each

1

year there have been some improvements'' (p. 115). The text concludes that
in spite of all these problems and in the face of criticism from ''un-American''
elements who do not want the people to become educated, ''the public schools
have gone steadily FORWARD'' (p. 115).

A reading of this text always generates a variety of responses on the part
of my students, and whenever I think every possible reading or interpretation
of the text has been presented, someone invariably presents a new interpretation,
one I had not thought of before. This, in itself, provides an important metaphor
for democratic education. We might say that democratic education involves a
way of seeing things in a new light and refusing to be limited or constrained
by past readings of texts. Democratic teaching also is based on acknowledging
that different readings of texts are not only possible but desirable, and that no
one (including the teacher) can claim to have an ''authorized'' or ''official''
reading that we all have to subscribe to. Each student brings something new to
the reading and the making of meaning, and by sharing our readings in dialogue
with others, we develop a more complex and critical understanding.

What, then, are some of the possible readings of this anonymous text from
the early Progressive era? One thing many students note is that the text seems
very idealistic and naive, and that it paints an overly rosy view of public schools.
Students often point out that the text is too optimistic about all the wonderful
things public schools are doing, and how it represents everything as getting
bigger and bigger and better and better. Students are far less likely to paint a
rosy view of public schools, and no one thinks of things as getting better any-
more. For example, one of the first things students often comment on is that
the text suggests that with progress, more and more libraries will be built and
prisons will disappear. Quite the opposite seems to be happening, they conclude.

The optimism of the text reflects more than the optimism of an earlier era.
One reason it is so upbeat and positive has to do with the fact that it is a sort
of advertisement for public education. This text was published in a journal that
was the major ''voice'' of the professional educational establishment during the
first half of this century. It thus represents the interests of the profession, and
more particularly the interests of important power brokers in the profession, in
''selling'' a very positive image of public education both within the profession
and to the general public. This raises an important point in all textual analysis.
In reading texts, it is important to know something about how the text was produced and deployed and for what purposes. Texts are not neutral depositories
of knowledge. Rather, they are ''discursive practices,'' discourses that also and
at the same time are involved in advancing certain agendas and representing
certain interests.

In discussing the *NEA Journal* text, I typically point out that in 1923, the
year this editorial was printed, the NEA was a professional association thoroughly dominated by male administrators, with teachers (most of whom were
women) subordinated and largely silenced within the association's leadership.

This led one teacher in my class to remark, "Now I understand why the picture depicts the schools as a phallic symbol, a skyscraper." Perhaps not surprisingly, this metaphor or symbolism had eluded me, as a male, until it was pointed out to me by a woman. What I saw, at least prior to learning to see the building as a symbol of masculine power, was a building that was corporate and industrial and thus a symbol of the emergence of corporate models of managing public education. Of course, the building is at one and the same time both of these metaphors and symbols, for corporate and patriarchal power have not been easily separable in this century. Several students have called our attention to the fact that this is a text that is decidedly silent about racial diversity in the United States. To many white students, this reading of the text is not self-evident. Why, they ask, does the text need to mention race? Do we always have to bring race into everything? The answer, of course, is that race, class, gender, and sexuality are involved in organizing our culture in profound and far-reaching ways, and texts represent that culture. They cannot not be there. This often leads us into a discussion of how "normalizing" texts serve to make those at the margins either invisible or represented as the deficient Other. Finally, a few students typically point out that the text depicts knowledge and the learning process in a very "fact-oriented" or "cut-and-dried" fashion, as if all they (teachers) did was deliver facts to students. There is no conception in this text of students as active makers of meaning, as constructors of truths and knowledge themselves; and there is no conception of truth as something produced within discourses and practices that serve some interests rather than others. Democratic education, like democratic culture, cannot be built upon reductionistic conceptions of knowledge and truth such as those represented in this text.

After having thoroughly deconstructed this Progressive-era text, at least one student in each class typically raises a final, half-tentative reservation—or I voice it myself: "But, isn't it important to believe in the ideals represented in the text, even if we haven't achieved them?" Most of us have been drawn to public education and to teaching because of our commitments to certain democratic ideals, which are still there beneath our cynical veneers. The trouble is that while we may believe public education should serve to advance some vision of a better society, most of us are not very hopeful that this will happen. We also lack a clear sense of how we might begin to "reinvent" public education in democratic ways in order to respond to rapidly changing developments that seem beyond our control. These are, I think, symptoms of a larger problem. We risk losing a sense of progress toward the fuller realization of the democratic project.

PROGRESS, PROGRESSIVISM, AND POSTMODERNISM

One of the characteristics of this new age we are entering, which often is called the postmodern, is this growing cynicism about modernist stories of progress—

a cynicism and skepticism that run especially deep among those most drawn to democratic values and struggles for social justice. Much of this is for the good, I think; for a critique of the idea of progress as it has been given meaning in dominant discourses of school reform in this century is necessary if we are to reappropriate the idea of progress to make it serve democratic purposes. Skepticism about progress at this time also is related, I think, to our increasing sophistication in deconstructing popular cultural texts to show how they represent, for example, race or gender identity, and how they tell particular stories that privilege the voices of some and silence others. This way of theorizing about culture also may be called postmodern. Among other things, postmodernism represents a way of seeing culture in ways that are much more complex and that reveal the power relations and interests behind constructs such as "progress."

This is related to a growing distrust of the power of the state and grand "meta-narratives" of state reform designed to impose a uniform and unifying system of controls from the top down. One of the lessons to be learned from a history of the twentieth century is that authoritarian regimes often are built and sustained through campaigns to rebuild the nation according to some utopian or dystopian vision. Early in this century, in his dark, foreboding satire on modernism and progress entitled *Man and Superman* (1903), George Bernard Shaw observed that "we have not sufficient energy" as a people to build the utopian societies that are to be the end rewards of progress. So if such societies are to be constructed, he concluded, it will have to be through "intolerant wilfulness and brute force" (p. 231). As it turned out, this was a prophetic vision. The Soviet Union and Nazi Germany were both built around the idea of rebuilding culture according to a master plan for progress. I do not mean to imply that progressive reform movements in public education in the United States have served authoritarian interests to anywhere near the same extent. However, it is the case that tendencies toward the concentration of power in the state and its various bureaucratic agencies have been apparent in the United States as elsewhere during the twentieth century, and progressive reforms have encouraged these developments. Postmodernism in this sense represents a healthy distrust of reform schemes that invest too much power in the state or that homogenize away local differences and local controls.

At the same time, it is important, I think, that we not abandon the idea of progress entirely. For one thing, powerful interest groups are working to reinvent public education consistent with their own vision of progress. If democratic progressives are not able to articulate forceful new stories of progress in education, based on new myths, metaphors, and visions of what could be, then other, less democratic and more oppressive stories of progress will win the day. Furthermore, some democratic progress has been made in education, and we are witnessing efforts to roll back this progress. Efforts aimed at increasing equality of opportunity for females and racial minorities, along with efforts to make the curriculum more multicultural and less patriarchal, are examples of the kinds of reforms democratic groups have struggled hard and long for. While these reforms certainly are limited in their impact on a system that continues to play such a central role in the production and reproduction of inequality, they are worth preserving and extending, but all of these gains are likely to be rolled back if conservative forces are able to define what counts as progress in the crucial years ahead. The question is not whether progress is still possible. The question is, Whose vision of progress will prevail as we enter an uncharted new century?

THE PROGRESSIVE ETHOS IN SCHOOL REFORM

Progressivism in education has never been a unified project or movement. Early in this century, almost everyone who opposed a traditional liberal arts curriculum and who believed that education should be oriented toward the needs of youth in modern society considered themselves progressives. Progressivism as a social and educational reform movement spanned the political spectrum from left to right; and almost all mainstream educational reformers and policy makers invoked the language of progressivism. In the 1950s, the term *progressivism* was stigmatized by conservatives who associated it with "permissive" forms of teaching and with an "un-American" emphasis on cooperation over individual competition (Cremin, 1961; Spring, 1989). This was a narrow use of the term *progressive* and one not very consistent with mainstream progressivism; but the association began to stick. Since then, mainstream educators for the most part stopped calling themselves progressives. However, they have continued to be progressive in the sense that they are oriented toward finding ever more effective methods of increasing student achievement levels and linking education to the reconstruction of society according to particular visions of the "good society." Consequently, I will refer to dominant reform discourses in education at this time as progressive, even if that term most often is associated with educational reform in the first half of this century. In continuing to use the term *progressive* to refer to mainstream reform discourses, I want to call attention to the fact that while things are changing in public school reform as we enter a "postmodern" historical era, reform discourse still is organized around the same basic stories of progress, stories that participate in the construction of social inequality and that privilege some voices just as they silence others.

Probably the most influential discourse and practice of progressivism in education in this century is what I will call *economic progressivism*. Its utopian vision is of a society of happy workers and "team players," each person doing his or her part to maximize productivity and lower costs; and it is a society in which politics has been replaced by management theory and "cost-effectiveness'' analysis. Throughout the twentieth century, economic progressivism has used two primary metaphors to advance reform agendas in public education. One of these is the metaphor of student as worker, which emphasizes the schools' role in preparing young people to be productive workers. While this metaphor typically is associated with a rationale that emphasizes meeting the needs of young people, it also and increasingly is associated with an economic rationale that suggests that for the United States to maintain or regain its economic preeminence, workers need to be more productive and skilled. A second metaphor economic progressives have drawn upon is that of the school as a business. This metaphor provides a rationale for arguing (among other things) that public schools be reorganized so that they are run more cost-effectively, that superintendents model themselves after corporate managers, that the ''product'' of the educational process be clearly defined, and (recently) that public education be privatized and students and parents treated as ''customers.''

Throughout most of the century, economic progressivism has tied these two metaphors—student as worker and school as a business—to an industrial, factory metaphor of educational productivity. This has translated into a heavy emphasis on standardization, regimentation, and role formalization. As we move into a postindustrial, information age, economic progressivism continues to be the most influential discourse of school reform, although it now is linked to the economic realities of a more two-tiered labor force, with basic skills emphasized for entry-level high school graduates. The school is still viewed as a business, run either efficiently or inefficiently, but more emphasis is now placed on cooperation, collaboration, teamwork, and site-based management. As consumerism has become more important in defining who we are, neoconservative economic progressives have begun to draw upon free market metaphors to support voucher systems of privatized schooling (Bridges & McLaughlin, 1994; Chubb & Moe, 1990).

Economic progressivism has led school reform in some very undemocratic directions in this century, since both the labor market that students are being prepared for and the organizational models that have undergirded school reform efforts, are characterized by great inequities of power. Of course, there is nothing inherently wrong with some limited use of economic metaphors in school reform. Within a society in which there were many more good jobs (in terms of both pay and nature of work) it would make sense for the public schools to help prepare young people for entry into the world of work—although this should hardly be the primary goal of public education. However, within the context of an economy of great inequality, with many low-skill, low-wage jobs, strict adherence to an economic rationale for curriculum reform puts public education in the position of preparing a good many young people for socioeconomic disempowerment. Economic rationales also may be linked to a ''hidden curriculum'' of schooling that emphasizes conformity to work norms and authority relations.

How do we account for the fact that economic progressivism has been such an influential discourse of school reform? One of the reasons is that business elites exercise a good deal of direct influence over the formulation of state policy through various lobbying groups and policy think tanks, such as the Brookings Institution and the Business Roundtable. Beyond this direct influence over policy making, which is linked to large financial contributions to both major political parties, economic progressives have been effective in articulating a ''commonsense'' discourse on reform that is designed to appeal to many traditional American values, including hard work and high standards, along with nationalistic desires to surpass foreign economic competitors and individualistic desires to get a good job.

However, elite economic models and ideologies have not been the only ones to exert a powerful influence over state educational policy in this century. Closely related to the project of economic progressivism, but representing distinctively different interests and perspectives, has been a project that I will call *disciplinary progressivism*. I use ''disciplinary'' in the sense in which Michel Foucault used it, in his history of the modern Prison, *Discipline and Punish* (1979) and in his other works. Perhaps more than anyone else, Foucault is identified with the postmodern critique of progress, and his historical studies of the rise of the human science disciplines (medicine, psychiatry, sociology, psychology, etc.) in the early modernist era are designed explicitly to challenge the conventional story of progress. He suggests that the human science disciplines, rather than being servants of the public, emerged as part of a project by the sovereign or state to impose greater order and discipline upon the body politic in order to make individuals at once more docile and productive. The human science disciplines also played an important role in legitimating this power over individuals as being ''in their own best interests'' and as the end product of a rational decision-making process by experts. The story Foucault tells, consequently, is one that links modernism to the erosion of human freedom and diversity. At best, we can say that one form of power over individuals and groups (as represented, for example, by the authority of the church) began to give way to another form of power (represented by the state and the authority of expert knowledge).

This critique of modernism and the rise of disciplinary power are beginning to influence the way we ''see'' and interpret the rise of mass public education in this century and the increasing power of the state over local school districts and over individual students' lives (Kohli, 1995; Popkewitz, 1991). Schools have, in effect, been among the primary agencies of ''normalizing'' power in the twentieth century, involved in the production of well-disciplined, ''well-adjusted" citizens and workers who conform to the hierarchical power relations and norms of modern life. By the 1950s, that decade of the official celebration of conformity, mainstream progressivism even used the language of "life adjustment" to describe the purpose of public education, which implied, among other things, learning how to work cooperatively with others, how to assume one's expected role in the nuclear family, how to use one's leisure time "constructively," and so on (Cremin, 1961; Spring, 1989). We also can see how the power of the professional educational "expert" has grown as public schools have assumed a more important role in producing the modern subject. This power has been legitimated by linking it to the supposedly "objective" and thus politically disinterested knowledge derived from the educational sciences. At the same time, claims that educational decisions are primary ones that require specialized expertise have been used to exclude other voices—including those of students, of parents, and of community groups—from the decision-making process.

Disciplinary progressivism, as part of a dominant modernist project of producing the docile, disciplined, productive subject, also has been involved in constructing boundaries between the "normal" and the "abnormal" and bringing the latter under the more effective "gaze" of power. While educational reforms in this century have claimed to be about constructing "universalistic" norms, they in fact have taken middle-class values as a standard of normality, along with "whiteness," maleness, and heterosexuality. Those marginalized in the process of constructing this norm are apprehended in terms of their deficiencies and limited potentials. This form of progressivism has been associated with a number of related "scientific" theories of learning, including (1) a theory of cognitive development that has been used to argue that since poor, inner-city youth are developmentally behind middle-class, suburban, white students, they cannot be pushed too far academically; (2) a cultural deficit or cultural pathology theory that presumes most poor and/or nonwhite students come from homes and communities that leave them emotionally crippled and unable to learn, and (3) a skill deficit theory that presumes these students need to be drilled in basic skills rather than challenged with higher-order thinking skills. These psychological theories that continue to undergird much curriculum reform discourse and practice, and that legitimate tracking and ability-grouping practices that reproduce class and race inequality, are major impediments in the path of democratic educational renewal.

Finally, we may associate disciplinary progressivism with an approach to reform, again particularly for schools serving the poorest, most marginalized students, that is heavily involved in finding ever more effective and efficent means of disciplining and "managing" student bodies. In this regard, public schools have modeled themselves not so much on the factory as on the modern, efficiently organized and operated prison. It may be, after all, as Foucault implies, that the prison is one of the most powerful metaphors in modern society. It enacts a very modern ritual in which the individual is placed under the perfect "gaze" of an all-knowing power at all times—a regimented body, told when to get up, when to eat, what work to do and how to do it, when to stop and when to start. All of this disciplining and punishing gets couched in the professional language of rehabilitation and preparing the inmate to re-enter society as a well-adjusted, productive citizen. In postmodern times, the metaphor of the school as prison, is, I am afraid, becoming even more influential. The prison or fortress inner-city school of the near future may be a site where "panoptic" control is exercised over student inmates at all times through the use of television cameras in halls, where metal detectors and security guards are everywhere, where students are efficiently herded from place to place through a system of bells and buzzers, where disruptive students are effectively isolated in individualized "time-out" rooms, and where resistant students move efficiently from the school's internal disciplinary apparatus to the juvenile court system. If our urban communities become even more socially and economically marginalized in the years ahead, and if schools continue to be heavily involved in the disciplining and punishment of resistant student bodies, then there is a very real possibility that the distinctions between penal and educational professionals, between prisons and schools, may begin to blur.

While economic and disciplinary progressivism have been the most powerful forces shaping public school reform in this century, we might distinguish yet another strand of progressivism that has exercised some influence in recent years—what I will call *process progressivism*. As I indicated earlier, the label "progressive" began to be stigmatized by conservatives in the 1950s; and much school reform discourse since then, while it has continued to be organized around economic and disciplinary stories of progress, has not called itself progressive. One of the effects of this is that by the late 1960s, progressivism began to be used to refer to a much narrower, if still influential, movement in public education—one associated with the "process approach" of Jerome Bruner (1960) and others, in which students "discovered" knowledge through carefully guided "hands-on" investigations. In some ways, this variety of progressivism has some real democratic potential. Students are recast as active learners, learning and doing are not artificially separated, and efforts are made to make learning relevant to the interests of students. Nevertheless, I want to differentiate this form of process progressivism from democratic progressivism on two counts. First, process progressivism fails to contextualize the "discovery" of knowledge within a broader set of social projects having to do with the fuller realization of a democratic vision. Without a broader project or vision, process progressivism has been easily assimilated into dominant reform discourses. For example, process progressivism as a reform movement in the late 1950s and early 1960s was closely associated with the rise in power of the military-industrial complex in the state, which saw in "discovery learning" a way of training a new generation of mathematicians and scientists who could discover new weapon technologies. In the 1990s, federal support for process progressivism continues, where it is now referred to as "constructivism." As before, constructivism is primarily a reform movement in math and science education, although the discovery of new knowledge in math and science is now related to economic growth rather than military preparedness. Second, "process approach" reforms often have encompassed a developmental theory of the child that may be used to legitimate a hands-on approach for lower-ability-group students that does not push them to think abstractly, based on the presumption that these students are not developmentally ready for abstract reasoning (Delpit, 1995; Walkerdine, 1994). In this form, process progressivism has been implicated in tracking practices. Thus, process progressivism, while consistent with democratic progressivism in some ways, has not provided a real alternative to economic and disciplinary progressivism.

DEMOCRATIC PROGRESSIVISM IN EDUCATION

I want to define *democratic progressivism* as a historical approach to public school reform (including reforms affecting the organization and governance of schools, the curriculum, and teaching) grounded in a democratic vision of a more equitable, just, and caring society. Of course, like the other strands of progressivism in education I have identified, there has been no movement in education that explicitly calls itself democratic progressive, and by using this category I mean to refer to a number of diverse perspectives and traditions that are changing somewhat as we enter the postmodern age. For the most part, I think changes occurring in culture that might be grouped under the broad rubric of postmodernism are having a revitalizing effect on democratic progressivism and show promise of moving democratic discourse in encouraging directions and overcoming some of the limitations that have kept democratic progressivism a marginalized reform discourse in the twentieth century. At the same time, postmodernism poses new challenges to efforts to articulate a broad-based democratic discourse and movement for change in education and culture, for we are becoming more fragmented and divided as a culture and less inclined to build alliances and coalitions across our differences.

For purposes of analysis, I want to examine two overlapping but distinct currents of democratic progressivism in this century, what I will call *democratic pragmatism* and *social reconstructionism*. Each is associated with themes that have defined the democratic project in education; and while these themes need to be reappraised and adapted to a rapidly shifting cultural terrain, they provide a place to begin a democratic conversation and a tradition to build upon. Each tradition comes with its own limitations as well that have prevented it from exercising more influence over educational practice, although by interweaving or articulating these two traditions, I think it is possible to overcome some of these limitations.

What I want to call democratic pragmatism is a tradition in the United States that could well be (and often is) called Deweyan pragmatism, in reference to the leading figure in this tradition, John Dewey. Within the broad Deweyan pragmatic tradition in the United States, a number of themes surface, but I want to limit myself here to a brief discussion of several of these themes that I think are most pertinent to the articulation of a new democratic progressive discourse. These themes are organized around notions of a "reasonable" society, dialogue, the "common good," and "fuzzy utopianism."

Democratic pragmatism has its roots in the humanist vision of a "reasonable society." According to Stephen Toulmin (1990), humanists of the early Enlightenment meant several related things by "reasonable." "On the one hand," he writes, "this meant developing modesty about one's capacities. . . . On the other hand, it required toleration of social, cultural, and intellectual diversity" (p. 199). Reasonable people do not oppress one another, nor do they claim special privileges and rights they are unwilling to grant others. Reasonable societies are characterized by dialogue in which all voices are heard and none dominate; and learning how to dialogue with others becomes a major aim of democratic education (Burbules, 1993; Burbules & Rice, 1991). The vision of a reasonable society is radical to the extent that in order for such a multivocal dialogue to be established, existing power inequalities that privilege the voices of some and silence the voices of others will need to be challenged.

Democratic pragmatists from Dewey on also have generally been associated with the idea that the modern, democratic state (and public schools in particular) should serve the "public good" or the "common interest" (Dewey, 1916). This is a problematic theme, for as I just indicated, democratic pragmatists have recognized society as pluralistic, and the vision of a reasonable society is one in which no unified conception of the "public" can be said to prevail. In postmodern times, as culture becomes more fragmented and diverse, the idea of a unified "public interest" is becoming even more suspect. Nevertheless, like the idea of progress, the idea of a public interest is one that democratic forces abandon at great peril, even if we must fight overly unifying conceptions of the public. In recent years, the notion of a public good has been linked to communitarianism, a broad-based movement to reassert community values and rights in American public life (Barber, 1984; Etzioni, 1993). In its more conservative and authoritarian forms, communitarianism implies a reassertion of citizen responsibilities *over* citizen rights. As such, it represents a reaction against the growing diversity of U.S. culture and the assertion of rights by those marginalized in the dominant culture. In its more democratic progressive forms, communitarianism represents an effort to recognize difference and support the extension of individual and group-based rights, while at the same time calling for a renewal of community life that brings us together to support one another and learn from one another across our differences. Benjamin Barber (1984), for example, argues that "individual members are transformed through their participation in common seeing and common work, into citizens. . . . Citizens [maintain their] autonomy because their vision of their own freedom and interest has been enlarged to include others. . . . Their enlarged vision enables them to perceive in the common force the working of their own wills" (p. 232).

What does this imply in education? One thing it obviously implies is that public education needs to remain public. Democratic progressivism may be associated with public school choice plans, but not with efforts to privatize schools. For only within public schools is it possible to promote the type of democratic citizenry about which Barber speaks. Beyond keeping public schools public, we might expand students' awareness of and commitment to a public sphere of community life by breaking down some of the walls between the school and the community. One way of doing this is through "service learning," a form of education that involves students as active participants in projects in community service agencies (Moore, 1990). Some school districts are experimenting with service learning requirements for high school graduation. While this easily could become just one more graduation requirement, measured in hours of service, the idea of linking education much more directly to the reconstruction of community life is one that is very central and will need to be addressed in democratic agendas for renewal in the years ahead.

In their book, *The Good Society* (1991), Robert Bellah, Richard Madsen, William Sullivan, Ann Swidler, and Steven Tipton refer to the phenomenon, common across America in the 1980s, of public school systems faced with the prospect of admitting children with AIDS. This provided a concrete test of the kind of schools and communities superintendents, principals, teachers, parents, and community groups wanted to construct. According to the authors:

> Finding the right metaphor—seeing the child primarily as a human being in need of special compassion or primarily as a source of dangerous contamination—was critical to the outcome. . . . Those for whom the virtues of responsibility and care were determinative (and it is important that those virtues were located not only in them as individuals but in their sense of themselves as institutional representatives) thought not only that they had done the right thing but that they had taught their children a lesson more valuable than most of what they learn in the classroom. Those who, desiring to protect what was theirs, opted to reject the stigmatized child, remained closed, bitter, and defensive long after the event. Their children too had learned a lesson. (p. 13)

In this case, they had learned to stigmatize the Other and to place individual fears and prejudices above the kind of caring and connectedness required of democratic civic life. The reassertion of bonds of public connectedness and community will be difficult in times when traditional forms of community are rapidly disappearing and when our commercial culture encourages us to think only of "number one." However, the fact that most schools did ultimately admit children with AIDS and that most communities were drawn together to stand up against intolerance and fear also indicates that the spirit of community is very much alive in America, if it can be tapped into.

A final theme I want to explore that runs throughout the democratic pragmatic tradition is that progress must be made one step at a time, in reacting to concrete situations faced in the present. In this regard, Dewey's pragmatism is very consistent with recent postmodern perspectives that emphasize the openness and indeterminacy of the future, although Dewey tended to be more optimistic about the progress of history than postmodern theorists are. Dewey (1920/1988) observed that "the end [of history] is no longer a terminus or limit to be reached. It is the active process of transforming the existent situation. Not perfection as a final goal, but the ever-enduring process of perfecting, maturing, and refining is the aim in living." He referred to this attitude as one of "meliorism"—the belief that whatever conditions exist now, they may be bettered—and he associated this with an attitude of "reasonable hopefulness" (pp. 179–180). To some degree at least, this conception of progress—like postmodernism—is thus non-utopian. However, non-utopian does not imply anti-utopian. Richard Rorty (1989), working in the Deweyan tradition, talks of the pragmatic need to construct "fuzzy utopias," visions of a better, more humane future that are deliberately vague and imprecise yet provide us with some basis for advancing democratic agendas and some hope for a better tomorrow. He argues that to ask for more clarity and detail is, to use an extreme example, like "asking a fourth-century Athenian to propose forms of life for the citizens of a twentieth-century industrial society." Rather than assurance that we are headed in a specific direction toward a clear goal, pragmatism offers hope that we can reconstruct culture in ways that are more egalitarian, that expand the human potential, that increase the freedom of individuals to control their lives, and that bring individuals and groups together across their differences in building a common public life. Rorty (1989) concludes, "Hope—the ability to believe that the future will be unspecifiably different from, and unspecificably freer than, the past—is the condition of growth. That sort of hope was all that Dewey himself offered us" (p. 201). Hope rather than optimism is what must provide a foundation for democratic progressivism in new times, a hope that is enacted in concrete struggles currently being waged over the course and direction of American culture and education.

While democratic pragmatism focuses our attention on important themes that must be addressed in educational renewal, it, like all traditions, comes with some limitations that need to be acknowledged. By limitations I mean ways of understanding or "seeing" problems and situations that limit the capability of groups and movements to achieve their goals or further advance their purposes. One of the central limitations of democratic pragmatic discourse has been a tendency to presume that through dialogue and reasoning together we can arrive at a consensus as to the public good, supposedly without the need to organize political coalitions and power blocs or struggle over the meaning of the public good. Democratic pragmatism, then, does not come with an adequate theory of cultural struggle, and this limits its usefulness in forging a democratic progressive movement for change, since such movements are always constituted out of the struggles of the dispossessed to achieve freedom, equity, and social justice, and for the silenced to find a voice and be heard.

Another limitation of democratic pragmatic discourse has been a tendency to view the modern state and public education as generally serving democratic interests and working to counter "private" interests in the economy and elsewhere. While the state and public education have been open to democratic influences in this century, as I argued earlier, economic and disciplinary varieties of progressivism most often have gained the upper hand in shaping reform discourse. This also means that when democratic forces have been able to mobilize enough political support to ensure that certain reforms are adopted, much of the democratic potential of these reforms has been subverted through integration within the dominant discourse and practice in schools. Public education does need to be reformed, but only within the context of a broader project of democratization of the state. So long as the state is so heavily influenced by elite economic and bureaucratic interests, there will be limited room to make democratic progress within it. Given this fact, social movements working outside the framework of the state play an increasingly important role in postmodern society in advancing democratic progressive projects, and their influence is likely to increase in the years ahead.

If democratic pragmatism has tended toward educational reformism, the second tradition of democratic progressivism I want to examine—social reconstructionism—has set its sights on "transformative" and "liberative" change in culture and education. The common link between these two traditions is to be found in the work of Dewey. In *Democracy and Education* (1916), Dewey asserts that the aim of education is the reconstruction of experience, and that "the reconstruction of experience may be social as well as personal" (p. 78). By the 1930s, as America grappled with economic crisis and with the great inequalities of wealth and power that had come to characterize life in the United States, Dewey along with other leading progressives of the time began to actively assert the critical role of public education as part of a broad democratic project of social reconstruction. The members of this group, which included in addition to Dewey such established leaders in the field as William Heard Kilpatrick and John Childs, were often referred to as social reconstructionists. Together they published a journal, *The Social Frontier*, and co-authored a book edited by Kilpatrick called *The Educational Frontier* (1933) that were major social reconstructionist texts. This association between progressivism and social reconstructionism in the 1930s was one of the reasons conservatives in the 1950s branded progressives socialists and un-American.

Like progressivism in general, social reconstructionism resurfaced later— even if it did not always go by that name. By the late 1960s, a new generation of educators, brought up politically on the cultural struggles of that decade, was developing a new social reconstructionist discourse in education. This included the voices of militant young teachers in America's simmering urban ghettos like Jonathan Kozol, whose *Death at an Early Age* (1967) was an autobiographical account of teaching in Boston schools that was also a scathing indictment of a system that not only failed to care but actively oppressed inner-city children. By the mid-1970s, a new social recontructionist discourse was being forged in the academy, grounded primarily in a neo-Marxist theory of schooling in advanced capitalism. Among the organizing constructs or ideas that run throughout this diverse and changing tradition of social reconstructionism there are several that I want to highlight here: "transformative" change, cultural struggle, and the teacher as an engaged intellectual.

Within the social reconstructionist tradition, as within the Marxist tradition more generally, progress in society is understood less in terms of evolutionary change and more in terms of transformation from one historical era and form of social organization to another. Transformative conceptions of history are generally dialectical. That is, they understand culture in terms of struggle between opposing power blocs and ideologies, a struggle that ultimately ushers in a new synthesis and thus a new stage in history. Transformative changes involve a dramatic or radical redistribution of power and the emergence of fundamentally new ways of understanding things—similar to what Thomas Kuhn (1970) has called "paradigm shifts" in the natural sciences, involving, for example, a shift from a Newtonian to an Einsteinian conception of the universe. The language of transformative change links social reconstructionism to a more radical agenda than democratic pragmatism and to a clearer sense of direction in history, generally associated with a utopian vision. In education, transformative change generally implies a radical democratic restructuring of the organization and mission of public schools consistent with advancing agendas of social justice. Social reconstructionists link such transformative change in education to transformative change in other important cultural sites, including the state and the economy, since they recognize that schools are not autonomous agencies of change.

I indicated that transformative change is understood within the social reconstructionist tradition to result from struggle between opposing power blocs and commonsense belief systems or ideologies (Apple, 1993; Hall, 1990). This means that progress is, as it were, a by-product of cultural struggle. Sometimes people complain that there is too much conflict in our society and that it would be so much better if we could all just get along. We must resist this tempting myth of a society in which everyone gets along and there is no struggle, for it can lead only in authoritarian and oppressive directions and not democratic ones. Even in oppressive societies we find struggles simmering right below the surface. In democratic societies, struggle does not somehow end; it only gets channeled in proactive ways into the political process. Democratic struggle involves organizing, marching, forging political and social movements, and articulating agendas for change. This always occurs to at least some degree in opposition to others who are mobilizing to direct social progress in other directions.

By positioning education within the context of cultural struggle, social reconstructionists also have developed a critical pedagogy that views the teacher as an engaged, "transformative intellectual" rather than merely the facilitator of dialogue (Giroux, 1992, 1994). Education is understood to be an inherently political process, involving helping students "demystify" the everyday world that they inhabit to reveal both the power relations and interests that structure it and the commonsense beliefs that support such power relations and structures. The objective of such a critical pedagogy is, on one level, personal empowerment, particularly of those marginalized in society. By empowerment I mean here the capability, through self-reflection, to take control of one's life and direct it rather than be the hapless victim of circumstances. However, the purpose of critical pedagogy is always to locate personal empowerment within a broader context of the political and cultural empowerment of marginalized groups. This also and inevitably means locating it within the context of cultural struggles in which we cannot escape taking positions and where we are faced with the responsibility of becoming actively engaged in the remaking of self and culture.

Although the social reconstructionist tradition has contributed much to our understanding of democratic progress in education and culture, it has been limited in its own way. For example, while the notion of transformative change is useful in helping us move beyond mere reformism in education, it may promote a belief that little can or should be done to help make things better here and now, since such efforts would involve only tinkering with an oppressive system to make it hold together longer. This was precisely the situation that neo-Marxist scholarship had worked itself into in the 1970s, and this partially accounts for the pessimism that began to creep into leftist discourse at that time. What this viewpoint fails to understand is that transformative change rarely if ever comes in grand revolutions that sweep away the old and usher in the new. It comes by pushing the current system to its limits and by working to develop "counterhegemonic" or oppositional power blocs and discourses. Thus, if democratic pragmatism too often has lost sight of its vision by emphasizing pragmatic reformism, social reconstructionism too often has failed to develop a pragmatic politics and has tended to get bogged down in critique.

As for cultural struggle, until the past decade or so social reconstructionist discourse focused almost exclusively on class struggle. While class is one of the central axes of identity formation within advanced capitalist societies, it is not the only one; and on its own it does not provide an adequate base for building a democratic progressive movement. There are encouraging signs, however, that social reconstructionist discourse has begun to reflect the diverse politics of postmodern society, and cultural struggle now is most often understood in terms of the interrelatedness of class, race, gender, and/or sexual politics. Unfortunately, where once social reconstructionist discourse was overly unifying, now it risks becoming too fragmented and unable to find any common ground. Finding a middle ground between a politics of unity and a politics of separate agendas will not be easy in the years ahead, but it appears to be the path democratic progressives will need to tread. Finally, social reconstructionist approaches to pedagogy raise questions about the authority of the teacher in democratic education that are unresolved and probably unresolvable. Early reconstructionists came close to advocating that students be taught a very narrow "politically correct" version of the truth. More recently, the shift toward acknowledging multiple truths and the interrelatedness of our understanding of the truth with our class, race, gender, and sexual identities has resulted in a less directive role for the teacher. The emphasis is on helping students find their own voices through the production of autobiographical narrative (Grumet, 1988; McLaughlin & Tierney, 1993) and on the interpretation of popular cultural texts (including advertisements, TV shows, magazines, videos, etc.) to reveal how they represent culture and various identity groups in it (Giroux, 1994; McCarthy & Crichlow, 1993).

DEMOCRATIC PROGRESSIVISM AND POSTMODERN TIMES

We are, for better or worse, entering into new times in which many of our taken-for-granted beliefs about culture, self, truth, and reality are being challenged. These are also, as a consequence, unsettling times, which are characterized by a breakdown of established orders and disciplines, technological advances that have just begun to have an impact on our lives, a new postindustrial economy that is further separating the haves and the have nots, and a new multicultural society that is pushing us toward redefining ourselves as a nation and a people. Unsettling times such as these are times of great opportunity as well as danger. Democracy may be re-visioned, and democratic social movements and political power blocs may articulate a bold new direction through this postmodern cultural terrain. However, nothing guarantees that that will happen. Given that democratic progressivism has had such a limited influence on educational practice in public schools in the twentieth century, is there much reason to hope that things might be different in the future?

I think the answer to that question is a tentative "yes." For as I have already indicated, democratic pragmatic and social reconstructionist traditions in the United States provide a solid base upon which to build a new democratic progressive discourse. In a way, each helps overcome some of the limitations associated with the other. Democratic pragmatism reminds us that progress must be built one step at a time, while social reconstructionism reminds us that we must not lose sight of our vision. Democratic pragmatism reminds us that through dialogue we can become more "reasonable" and better able to appreciate the perspectives of others, and social reconstructionism reminds us that dialogue alone cannot build a democratic society and that there is a time to "take sides." This suggests that a new democratic progressive discourse might be able to overcome many of the problems that limited its influence in the twentieth century, if it is able to more effectively articulate or interweave these two distinct traditions, acknowledging the tensions between them.

However, for this potential to be realized democratic progressivism will need to articulate responses to the struggles currently being waged over the "reinvention" of public education in a postmodern culture. In turn, such engagement will require a reawakening of the democratic spirit, including the spirit of progress and hope. Democratic progressivism for postmodern times, Paulo Freire (1994) writes, must be based on "avoiding both the illusions of an idealism that ascribes a power to education that it does not have, and the mechanistic objectivism that denies any value to education until after there is a revolution" (p. 200). It is in this spirit, I think, that we best proceed; and it is to a politics of cautious hope that this book is dedicated.

2

Public Education in Changing Times

No form of life does or can stand still; it either goes forward or it goes backward, and the end of the backward road is death. Democracy as a form of life cannot stand still. It, too, if it is to live, must go forward to meet the changes that are here and are coming.
—John Dewey, The Problems of Men

THERE HAS BEEN MUCH talk in the past few years of changes that are fundamentally reshaping culture, the implications of which we have just begun to grasp. Some of this talk may be attributed to the fact that as a culture we are approaching an important marker, the year 2000. Yet, this is an arbitrary number, and one that is Eurocentric and Christian as well. After all, in the Chinese calendar and the calendars of other peoples in the world, the Christian year 2000 is just another year. Still, the belief that we are entering into "new times" or a "new age" is at least partially self-fulfilling. It is also the case that technological changes associated with the emergence of an information culture are accelerating at this point in history as the computer begins to transform our lives and the organization. Meanwhile, the postindustrial economy is going through a great restructuring in the face of all of these changes, and one of the results is a widening of class divisions that threatens to make democracy in America more formal than "real." Within another 2 decades, the America most of us grew up in will be a fading memory. How can we respond in democratic ways to these changes reshaping American culture and affecting public education? That is the question I want to address, in some tentative ways, in this chapter.

In suggesting how we might proceed in fundamentally rethinking democratic progressive approaches to education consistent with postmodern cultural developments, I want to draw upon insights from three distinct but interrelated strands of postmodern theorizing. The first of these is associated with theorists of the so-called "new social movements," including Ernesto Laclau and Chantal Mouffe (1985), Alberto Melucci (1989a, 1989b), Alain Touraine (1988), and

A somewhat modified version of this chapter was published as "Making Progress: Progressive Education in the Postmodern" by D. Carlson, 1995, *Educational Theory, 45*, pp. 337–358.

others. These theorists point to the growing importance of relatively autonomous social movements of identity and lifestyle, on both the political left and right, that are involved in defining not only who we are but what our politics are as well. A second postmodern discourse I examine, associated with neo-Marxist theorists of "post-fordism," focuses our attention on the economic and technological forces that are driving many of the shifts in culture designated as postmodern. Specifically, I want to comment on shifts toward a "networked" and decentralized organization, new forms of consumerism that emphasize choice, and a two-tiered labor force (Hall, 1990). A final strand of postmodern discourse I want to examine is associated with the work of Michel Foucault (1979). My concern is with Foucault's analysis of "normalization" as a modernist project, involving the construction of disciplined subjectivities and bodies, and more particularly his analysis of recent trends in normalization associated with individualizing, totalizing, and "pastoral" power. All of these strands of postmodern theorizing have some important implications for how we rethink democratic progress at this historical juncture; my concern is with teasing out some of these implications.

I mean to take none of these postmodern theoretical "lenses" as providing in itself a sufficient basis for articulating a democratic progressivism attuned to postmodern cultural developments. Rather, I mean to suggest that democratic discourses on progress need to be articulated by looking at culture through multiple lenses and seeing what each has to reveal along with what each blinds us to. At this point, conservative forces have been far more effective at articulating postmodern shifts in culture with their own agendas for progress, and this suggests the need for some serious rethinking of what democratic progress should mean in these unsettling new times.

NEW SOCIAL MOVEMENTS AND THE POLITICS OF EDUCATION

Theorists of the new social movements have argued that, beginning somewhere in the 1960s, politics in advanced capitalist societies began to become less class-based and less tied to major political parties. The mass media, particularly television, along with the advent of computerized mailings, made it possible for more groups to organize outside of parties and advance their own autonomous agendas. Furthermore, many of these new social movements were organized around identity, lifestyle, and values, and their concerns went far beyond gaining a bigger piece of the economic pie. By addressing issues of values, lifestyles, and identity that affect us in our everyday relations with others, new social movements have focused our attention on the "politics of everyday life" and the way we organize our relations with others. Also, social movements increasingly provide new forms of community in a society in which traditional conceptions of community have virtually broken down. According to Melucci (1989a), one of the leading theorists of the new social movements, the process of establishing a social movement involves "activating relationships among the actors, who communicate, negotiate and make decisions; and . . . making emotional investments which enable individuals to recognize themselves in each other [and] . . . participate in the process of identity building" (p. 35). Social movements are not easily located on the kind of modernist political map that places everything on a neat line between left and right. Each movement raises its own issues and pursues fairly autonomous agendas, so that linkages between movements are provisional, unstable, and situational.

Nevertheless, it is still possible to identify some social movements as generally to the left of center in their concerns. These include movements that represent the empowerment and civil rights agendas of groups marginalized by their racial, gender, sexual, or other identities—what are sometimes called "identity politics" movements (Bromley, 1989). Closely related to these movements are struggles organized around "body politics," involving the assertion of rights having to do with control over one's body (including sexual, reproductive, and abortion rights) (McLaren, 1988). Environmental, or "green politics," movements also may be positioned on the political left, since they challenge the unrestricted power of economic forces to exploit the natural environment. Most theorists of the new social movements have preferred to emphasize the influence of "progressive" social movements. However, New Right movements arguably have been just as influential, or more so in some cases, in pushing their agendas in the state and among the public. Most New Right movements in the United States are linked through a common fundamentalist Christianity, including the "right to life" movement, "family values" groups, groups opposed to "special rights" for homosexuals, and so on. These groups share with many progressive groups a sense of "things out of kilter," including a de-spiritualization of the world. Their response to the moral and spiritual crisis of modern society, however, is to seek a return to a romanticized, simpler, premodern past where everyone supposedly knew his or her place in life and unquestioningly accepted conventional moral authority. In this regard, they may be considered "backlash" movements against the limited progress made in challenging traditional gender roles and sexual mores over the past few decades and are positioned in opposition to identity and body politics movements.

Both major political parties have been influenced by political realignments going on in American society. In fact, the "conservative restoration" in American politics that occurred in the 1970s and 1980s relied on New Right movements representing fundamentalist Christians to form a hegemonic or governing power bloc (Schor, 1986). During the Reagan era in particular, this translated into support for prayer in the public schools, changes in science textbooks to make them more consistent with fundamentalist Christian teachings on "scientific creationism,'' ''just say no,'' and ''sex respect'' approaches to sexuality education that preach abstinence outside of heterosexual marriage. To appeal to the so-called ''Reagan Democrats'' and other working-class whites concerned that minorities and women were making too many advances, neoconservatives supported a rollback of affirmative action commitments, reasserted the primacy of a Eurocentric curriculum, and called for more law and order in urban schools. While the influence of New Right constituencies in shaping the neoconservative educational reform discourse in the 1970s and 1980s was considerable, we must be careful not to overstate their influence. Support for reforms sponsored by New Right movements was more often rhetorical than substantive, and New Right concerns effectively were insulated from the core neoconservative reform agenda, which was most influenced by a corporate discourse. Business and economic constituencies defined much of the language of educational reform (''excellence,'' ''higher standards,'' ''educational productivity,'' ''accountability,'' ''output-based learning,'' etc.), and their interests and agendas were not always consistent with those of the New Right. In 1992, the split between the New Right and the established business-oriented factions of the Republican party resulted in the splintering of this power bloc.

Meanwhile, the emergent neoliberal power bloc and reform discourse in the 1990s has been dependent on an uneasy alliance between movements representing African Americans, women, gays and lesbians, and environmentalists, along with liberal elements of the business community and the traditional liberal constituency of organized labor. The Clinton administration's strategy to this point has been based on both courting the new social movements and publicly distancing itself from them in order to appear not beholden to ''special interests'' (Peters, 1993). Certainly, neoliberalism has provided a somewhat more supportive environment for those who have sought to use public education to counter gender and racial inequalities, teach more tolerant and progressive views of human sexuality, and promote environmental ethics and values. In most ways, however, the Clinton administration's educational policy appears similar to the Bush administration's and is most influenced by an economic rationale. It ties this rationale to ''War on Poverty'' approaches to meeting the needs of all children, such as Head Start, but these programs are chronically underfunded and still take for granted a ''deficit'' theory of the child.

What, then, might provide a framework for building a ''counterhegemonic'' progressive educational policy? I want to use the notion of counterhegemony to refer to the active production of an oppositional movement or power bloc within a society that challenges the dominant power bloc for leadership in the state and ''civil society,'' that is, everyday institutional life. Modernist interpretations of counterhegemony understood it exclusively or primarily in terms of the mobilization of a working-class movement and power bloc. Postmodernism, to the extent that it is characterized by a movement away from unified oppositional politics, calls for the forging of a quite different type of power bloc. Probably the most influential theorists to address these issues have been Laclau and Mouffe, and the brunt of their argument in *Hegemony and Socialist Strategy* (1985) is that a democratic counterhegemony may be mobilized at this point only around a "politics of difference." This implies that rather than construct an oppositional meta-narrative on change, a counterhegemony is to be constructed by interweaving or *articulating* the discourses of various semiautonomous movements on the democratic left in such a way that no discourse dominates and each social movement maintains its specific agenda and language of struggle. "This form of politics," they argue, "opens the way for a 'radical pluralist democracy,' one in which the gains of the democratic imaginary are extended to ever deeper domains through the maximum autonomization of spheres" (quoted in Escobar, 1992, p. 39). Thus, the only common organizing principles of such a counterhegemony would be respect for difference and allowing individuals and affinity groups the maximum possible freedom or "space" to define themselves. However, Laclau and Mouffe recognize that the maximization of freedom would be possible only within a social context in which existing inequalities of power and wealth were significantly countered, since disempowerment and economic deprivation inhibit some individuals and groups from exercising much freedom.

In education, this view of a democratic counterhegemony implies a number of things. Most important, it means moving educational discourse beyond a narrow economic rationale to seriously address concerns raised by identity politics, body politics, and environmentalist movements. Taking identity politics seriously means a curriculum and form of teaching aimed at helping those who have been marginalized by class, race, gender, sexual orientation, and other markers of difference to construct empowering identities that link them to collective, historical struggles for equity and freedom. The discourse of critical pedagogy, especially over the past few years, has reflected this new, postmodern, and multicultural conception of empowerment (Giroux, 1993; McLaren, 1992). Taking identity politics seriously also may mean—at least at the high school and postsecondary levels—that efforts have to be made to find space for different identity and affinity groups to be recognized to defend their rights and interests within the school community. It also may mean support for alternative "magnet" high schools oriented around particular identities—such as Afrocentric schools, girls' schools, gay and lesbian schools, and so on. Taking body politics seriously means supporting the rights of individuals to control their own bodies and desires, and this would translate into affirming the rights of students to have much broader access to information on homosexuality, contraception, abortion, AIDS and other sexually transmitted diseases, and so forth, so that they can make informed choices. Finally, taking environmentalism seriously in the school curriculum and everyday life of the school suggests an increased emphasis throughout the curriculum on an ethic of care, and along with this a challenge to what Martin Buber has called "I–It" relations, in which the Other, including the natural environment, is distanced from self and brought under an instrumental, exploitive gaze (Buber, 1958; Noddings, 1992).

Some theorists of the new social movements, such as Melucci (1989a), have argued that a primary role of the democratic, postmodern state should be to provide space for various social movements to organize and represent their interests and concerns directly and actually to participate in negotiating state policy with other interested social movements and groups. This raises important concerns in forging a democratic progressive educational policy. Progressivism in the modernist twentieth century was associated with the centralization and bureaucratization of decision making in the state and a tendency to make the decision-making process less visible and more technical and professional. To Melucci, postmodern democratic policy can help counter these tendencies by creating and funding "public spaces"—sites in the community in which various affinity groups and social movements could monitor state policy, formulate their own positions, and be represented in an ongoing dialogue with other social movements over state policy. Public spaces in education might include special foundations and commissions that represent diverse constituencies, ad hoc task forces designed to address particular educational problems, community forums on educational renewal, public "watchdog" groups, and so on. Aside from making public policy more visible and public officials more accountable, Melucci argues that public spaces would meet the need for both *representation* and *participation* of new social movements in forging state policy: "Representation means the possibility of presenting interests and demands; but it also means remaining different and never being heard entirely. Participation also has a double meaning. It means both taking part, that is, acting so as to promote the interests and needs of an actor [or interest group], as well as belonging to a system, identifying with the . . . community" (p. 174). In this sense, public spaces would allow individuals and groups to express their different perspectives and interests but also participate in dialogue across their differences that is aimed at formulating a democratic educational policy.

Social movement theories have some important implications for the construction of a democratic progressive discourse in education. One of the problems with these theories, however, is that while they help move politics and policy beyond a narrow focus on class, they do so at the risk of losing sight of class analysis altogether. Not only do they ignore or de-emphasize class as an important axis of identity formation, along with trade unionism as a social movement, but they also fail to see the close connections between class oppression and race and gender oppression. A democratic progressive educational discourse cannot afford to ignore or downplay class and political economic analysis. In a sense, we may view social movement theorists as providing a map of the postmodern that is consistent with the perspective of the new professional-managerial class. It celebrates freedom and autonomy without much regard for the growing number of those left beyond economically, politically, and culturally, who arguably have less freedom in the new, postmodern era. Melucci (1989a), for example, claims we are entering a "post-material society, in which the primary needs of the population are to a large extent satisfied" and where freedom *from* material wants is being replaced by freedom *of* choice as to how to live one's life (p. 177). This greatly exaggerates the extent to which material needs have been met within advanced capitalist societies such as the United States, particularly at a time when good industrial jobs are disappearing. A democratic progressive policy must, I believe, remain firmly grounded in a commitment to represent the interests of the economically disenfranchised in the new world order, and also to the reconstruction of work experiences in America so that work becomes an arena for self-enhancement rather than alienation. This is where theorists of post-fordism are useful.

OF FORDISM, POST-FORDISM, AND EDUCATION

In the mid- to late 1980s in Great Britain, a group of leftist scholars who began to refer to themselves as "New Times" theorists engaged in an extended dialogue on directions for leftist politics, parts of which were published in *Marxism Today* and in a book edited by Stuart Hall and Martin Jacques entitled *New Times* (1990). The New Times theorists sought to expand leftist politics to embrace new social movements of race, gender, sexuality, and environmentalism. They also argued for the central role of class struggle in building a counterhegemony, and they understood postmodernism, to use the language of Fredric Jameson (1991), as the new cultural logic of capital. That is, postmodernism in culture is related to structural and material transformations occurring in capitalism—transformations that New Times theorists characterized as post-fordist. The notion of post-fordism firmly embeds New Times theorists within that least deterministic and most poststructural tradition of Marxist discourse associated with the work of Antonio Gramsci. In an essay on "fordism" and "Americanism" written early in this century, Gramsci had observed astutely that advanced capitalist societies such as the United States were then entering a new historical era, one characterized by what he called "fordism" in tribute to the American "father" of the mass production factory, Henry Ford (Gramsci, 1971). Gramsci used "fordism" to refer, among other things, to changes in politics (including the emergence of an industrial trade union movement and the welfare state), consumerism (including the beginnings of a mass consumer society that drove industrialization), and the way public institutions were organized (including the acceptance of the factory as the model of the "efficient" organization). "Post-fordism'' has been used by New Times theorists in a similar way to refer to a whole constellation of changes associated with the current transformation of capital. I want to focus my comments on three major clusters of post-fordist changes that I think have the most direct implications for public education: new organizational and management styles, new forms of consumerism, and the restructuring of the labor force. In each case, my interest is in the impact these changes are already having in redirecting neoconservative and neoliberal state educational policy as well as their implications for rethinking democratic progress in education. Consistent with a Gramscian perspective, I wish to argue that these clusters of changes create a new ''playing field'' or terrain of battle upon which power blocs on both the right and left are having to reposition themselves.

New Organizational and Management Styles

As the United States and other advanced capitalist countries began moving into a postindustrial era in the 1960s, new kinds of organizations began to become visible on the economic landscape organized around computer and information technologies, such as those in California's ''Silicon Valley'' and elsewhere. One of the primary characteristics of these organizations has been a heavy reliance on knowledge production, that is, generating new product ideas, designing new production technologies, and creating new market strategies to stay ahead of the competition. This has meant investing in highly skilled workers and then ''empowering'' them to be creative, flexible, and adaptive; this also entails a renewed emphasis on teamwork and ad hoc groupings of workers charged with brainstorming ideas and coming up with unique solutions to problems. The decentralization of power in post-fordist organizations also is being driven by new computer technologies that allow firms to tailor products and services more specifically to meet individual client and customer needs, which can be identified and responded to at the local level. The computer, along with the contracting of services and parts of the production process that once were provided ''in house,'' is promoting a more networked organization that no longer has rigid organizational boundaries.

A whole new management discourse has emerged over the past decade that heralds these changes in cutting-edge, post-fordist organizations as nothing less than ''revolutionary.'' For example, Tom Peters, in *Liberation Management* (1992), advises managers to begin ''deconstructing the corporation'' by smashing hierarchies, empowering employees, encouraging workers to redesign their jobs, and looking to a feminist ethic of care to encourage collaboration and dialogue. New Times theorists, as one might expect, have been more skeptical about claims that capitalism is ''reinventing'' itself, at least in ways that involve a fundamental redistribution of power. For example, the trend toward decentralization within firms is occurring within the context of the continuing concentration of economic power and wealth in a relatively few multinational corporations; and top CEOs and their staffs hold more of the power over substantive decisions about what products and services to offer, where investments will be made in product development or marketing, and so on. Furthermore, the post-fordist economy is characterized by the growth of a large service sector in which jobs are relatively low skill and work continues to be highly rationalized. Still, New Times theorists have not been totally critical of these changes. They have, in fact, generally viewed the newer, more flexible, and decentralized organizational styles as providing ways of thinking about the delivery of public services that overcome some of the problems associated with modernist, top-down, bureaucratic, and welfare state approaches—the kinds of approaches that those on the left have emphasized throughout much of the industrial era.

When we look for ways in which these post-fordist organizational styles are beginning to influence school restructuring discourse, we do not have to look very far. Site-based management, one of the most widely heralded reform movements of the 1990s, provides one good example of post-fordist restructuring. Under various plans and proposals, local school councils—including representatives of teachers, school staff, parents, community agencies, and students—are "empowered" to make a broad range of decisions having to do with such things as the organization of the curriculum and instruction, the pacing of instruction and scheduling of various activities, in-school discipline policies, the hiring of principals, and the use of discretionary funds to purchase school equipment. The networked school also may be considered post-fordist, with its close working relationships with universities, foundations, and funding agencies; community social service agencies; and consortiums of schools—all of which are breaking down the rigid organizational boundaries that have been erected around public schools in this century. Even the postmodern language of "empowerment" has become as popular in the discourse of school restructuring over the past few years as in management discourse. Theorists such as Thomas Sergiovanni (1992), for example, talk about the shift from "power over" others to "power to" others in building an "empowered school community." Sergiovanni writes: "Power *over* emphasizes controlling what people do, when they do it, and how they do it. Power *to* views power as a source of energy for achieving shared goals and purposes" (p. 133). He also suggests that "power *to* . . . is an idea close to the feminist tradition, as are such ideas as servant leadership and community" (p. 135).

While I think that these shifts in the discourse of school restructuring have important democratic potentials that need to be pushed to their limits, at present school reforms based on the "new paradigm" embody the contradiction I noted above—namely, the tendency to promote greater decentralization of decision making and more collaboration within the context of increased state power over what goes on in local schools. For example, within the current context, site-based management involves contradictory tendencies. In some forms, it actually may represent an extension of state power since "empowering" local school councils means holding them accountable for producing "outcomes" determined at the state level. The fact that most current proposals for site-based management come from superintendents and state officials rather than those who supposedly are being empowered, suggests just how much change is being incorporated within a dominant, and dominating, reform discourse. Site-based management also may take on meaning within a human relations discourse aimed at more effectively managing discontent and motivating the involvement of those subordinated within the institution, including teachers, students, parents, and community groups. In such cases, the hidden concern is often with making subordinates *feel* more involved in important decisions, even if their input is not listened to. Finally, the "empowerment" of local school staff is being driven partially by central office cost-cutting concerns. That is, it represents a way of increasing teachers' and principals' workloads by assigning them more committee work and eliminating a middle range of jobs in the central office (including curriculum development and supervision). Of course, to the extent that teachers, principals, parents, and others begin to recognize that "empowerment" translates into little more than an intensification of labor, they may begin to ask, to paraphrase Elizabeth Ellsworth (1989), "Why doesn't this feel empowering?" Thus this contradiction at least opens up the possibility of beginning a dialogue on what a more "real" or substantial empowerment would entail in the way of changes in school organization and governance, curriculum, and pedagogy.

What, in a general sense, might democratic progressivism stand for within the current push for school restructuring? First, a progressive reform discourse would need to move beyond the narrow, output-based, managerial orientation that undergirds most current reform discourse. Rather than the language of site-based management and decentralization, for example, democratic progressives might invoke the language of participatory democracy and workplace democracy. This would need to be accompanied by a rethinking of the role of the state in establishing standards to which local schools are expected to conform. Instead of prescriptive standards tied to standardized testing, the state might require that local school districts engage representative constituencies in the community in a dialogue on educational renewal or find ways of making the curriculum more multicultural, making students more active learners, and so on. The state also might help schools get connected with regional and national consortia of schools trying out various approaches to school democratization. Assessment of a school's effectiveness in meeting such state standards could be made part of the ongoing local dialogue on educational renewal. Within the school, the empowerment of teachers and their involvement in the dialogue on school change can, I believe, be facilitated only by reconfiguring teachers' work in ways that free up much more of their time during the day. This, in turn, is preconditioned on viewing students as active, empowered learners who are not dependent on ongoing teacher direction and supervision. Obviously, the current role that public schools assume as custodial and control institutions is inconsistent with moving very far in these democratic directions.

New Forms of Consumerism

Aside from changes in the way organizations are structured and managed, postfordism implies a renewed emphasis on consumer choice and product differentiation, and on the design, packaging, and marketing of products to appeal to "targeted" consumer groups (Hall, 1990, p. 118). Television programming provides a prime example of these trends. Mass formula programming rapidly is being replaced by "market niche" programming, with each program designed to appeal to a particular market segment, organized around a particular image or representation of class, race, gender, and sexual identity. For a certain young, college-educated, white, male, heterosexual market niche, for example, commercialized identities are constructed primarily around sports, which is linked to popularity with beautiful women, which is linked to deodorants, "light" beer, and sporty mini-pickups. For the fundamentalist market niche organized by religious broadcasters, identity is constructed around representations of "traditional family values," working-class and "country" lifestyles, and the cultural war being waged to "save" America from "secular humanism," sexual "perversion," big government, and other evils. Not only are programs targeted to audiences defined by lifestyle and cultural values; the program itself becomes largely inseparable from the commercials wrapped around and through it. Over the past few years there has been a proliferation of commercial channels and programming aimed at market niches, boosted by the technological development of cable TV. As with shifts in organizational style, these trends toward the maximization of choice and toward a more differentiated market are deeply contradictory, however. As long as choice is defined exclusively or primarily in terms of selecting from among various commercial channels attempting to sell images and identities to highly fragmented consumer groups, more channels may mean only a more effective and insidious control over consumers. Still, it is clear that individuals desire more choice over all aspects of their lives in the postmodern era and that the extension of human freedom will require increasing individuals' choices and options. The issue, then, is *how* choice gets defined, and within which cultural discourse.

In recent educational reform discourse, the language of choice most commonly has been linked to a neoconservative social agenda. Under various "voucher" plan proposals, advanced originally during the Nixon administration and more recently during the Bush administration in the "America 2000" plan to "reinvent" public education, parents would receive lump-sum allotments to help subsidize the education of their children in private and/or religious schools outside the public school system (Bush, 1991). This neoconservative discourse on school choice is firmly grounded in a classical, free market philosophy, as represented in John Chubb and Terry Moe's influential study sponsored by the Brookings Institution, *Politics, Markets, and America's Schools* (1990). The authors begin with the presumption that individuals are motivated to maximize their interests and that given complete information about the choices available to them on the free market and the likely consequences of various choices, they will choose what best serves their interests. Free market choice supposedly "depoliticizes" control in education, according to Chubb and Moe (1993), since under the current system school officials " . . . come under intense pressure from social groups of all political stripes whereas in a choice system curriculum decisions would be made by consumers" (p. 144).

One of the problems with using consumer analogies in thinking about how we should organize public institutions is that, like the larger consumer society they seek to emulate, public institutions end up providing significant choices only to those consumers who can afford to pay a premium price, and reducing the real choices available to those without much consumer capital. Most voucher proposals are based on a rather dramatic cutback in funding to public education, so that the allotments parents received from the state would only partially subsidize the education of their children. Those at the bottom of the socioeconomic order would be the hardest hit and have the fewest options to exercise, since their allotments would pay only for a minimum education in overcrowded, poorly staffed "welfare schools." Another problem with a conception of choice grounded in a purely consumer discourse is that it encourages individuals to think about their interests in narrowly instrumental and material terms. Thus, if we move to a voucher system of public education we are likely to see advertisements for schools that boast of immediate job payoffs or higher SAT scores, that coach students to pass state proficiency tests for high school graduation, and so on. The broader and arguably more important purposes of public education, including the education of an informed and critical citizenry that is actively involved in the production, not just consumption, of culture, tend to get de-emphasized or ignored entirely when the focus is on maximizing instrumental goals such as higher test scores, increased personal status, and high-paying jobs.

Finally, neoconservative discourse on choice in education has been contradictory in that it has promoted greater consumer choice and the decentralization of decision making to individual parents and their children at the same time that it has worked to more effectively centralize control over educational outcomes through a system of national standards linked to standardized testing. In Chubb and Moe's (1990) ideal system of choice, "the state will be responsible for setting criteria that define what constitutes a 'public school' . . . [and] standardized testing will be needed to set standards'' (p. 148). State-mandated standardized testing has the effect of severely restricting not only what is taught in public schools, but how it is taught as well. What is taught most commonly is facts, figures, equations, and hard, objective truths that are to be mastered, rather than a process of critical thinking and meaning making, involving the engagement in dialogue over social issues and personal identity. How it is taught is through test-preparation drills and a skills-based curriculum that is narrowly focused on what is going to be on the test.

While choice in education, as I have said, has been given meaning predominantly within a neoconservative discourse about "reinventing" schools, neoliberals in the 1990s also have begun to talk about school choice, and in at least somewhat more progressive ways. For example, one of the books most often credited with helping shape policy within the Clinton administration is David Osborne and Ted Gaebler's *Reinventing Government; How the Entrepreneurial Spirit Is Transforming the Public Sector* (1992). Osborne and Gaebler endorse a public school voucher plan in which local school boards would issue "charters" to businesses, universities, and local community groups to run individual schools or consortia of schools. The authors maintain that if vouchers are limited to public schools and funding levels are kept high, equality of opportunity actually can be enhanced since "[the state] can simply equalize the funding for each individual—or even increase it for those with less income. This also removes the stigma of subsidies for the poor by allowing them to participate in the mainstream—to attend any school'' (pp. 185–186). Such neoliberal proposals potentially could go a long way toward advancing a democratic construction of educational choice. They do this by seeking to ensure that freedom of educational choice is something that everyone has an equal right to, regardless of income level. They also maintain the separation of church and state, so that public vouchers could not be used, for example, to support a network of fundamentalist Christian churches dedicated to preaching new right values and substituting "scientific creationism" for science.

Nevertheless, neoliberal proposals currently are limited in important ways as well. First, they are still linked to national standards established through standardized testing, which, as I have already indicated, restricts and instrumentalizes both what is taught and how it is taught. Second, neoliberal voucher proposals are based on the proposition that school choice plans would be funded so as to provide quality educational options to all, with extra funds provided to those families that fall below the average income level. Yet neoliberals have been paralyzed by a deepening fiscal crisis and concurrent disassembling of the welfare state, piece by piece. This points to the importance of linking democratic educational renewal to a reallocation of resources in the state that supports investing in public schools over the military, and in education rather than the construction of more prisons. Finally, neoliberal discourse on choice has remained largely grounded in free market, entrepreneurial rationales. Some elements of free market competition may be desirable in public education, and one of the advantages of a voucher choice plan is that it would help "weed out" some of the most oppressive and least effective public schools. However, the competition of the free market also would likely weed out many small, progressive schools—ones that did not promise to raise students' test scores so much as they promised to engage students' minds, or ones based on a low teacher-student ratio and personalized instruction rather than on a more "cost-effective" and profitable form of computerized instruction with a few teacher's aides monitoring more than 100 students. Democratic choice means ensuring that diverse choices are made available and that students receive personalized attention, and this means restrictions on the free market.

The Restructuring of the Labor Force and Work

As the United States and other advanced capitalist societies have undergone deindustrialization since the late 1950s, a new postindustrial labor force has emerged, one that is highly fragmented, relatively unorganized, and more two-tiered than before, with racial minorities and women overrepresented in the larger, lower tier of service industry and clerical jobs that no longer provide a salary that can support more than one person at or above the official poverty level. Unfortunately, most high school graduates entering the labor force are limited to these jobs. Meanwhile, the number of high-skill jobs requiring a college education also has increased over the past 2 decades, although this sector of the labor force has not grown nearly as rapidly in actual numbers of jobs as has the lower tier (Kennedy, 1993; Uchitelle, 1990). These are the so-called "yuppie" jobs in the new high tech firms I talked about earlier—such as jobs in computer programming, the design and engineering of new computer technologies, and the production and marketing of products for specialized market niches. Largely as a result of the restructuring of the labor force around these two highly inequitable tiers, the disparity in earnings between young people with a high school diploma and those with a college degree increased by almost 50% between 1973 (the year the disparity was at its lowest point) and the end of the 1980s. From the post-World War II era until 1973, the median income of 25- to 34-year-old males with a high school diploma rose from around $14,500 to $24,500 (in constant 1987 dollars). After that year, the year of the Arab oil embargo and the symbolic beginning of the postindustrial age, the median income of that particular segment of workers declined steadily to about $18,400 in 1987—a net loss in income of 25%. Male high school dropouts experienced an even greater decline in earnings in the 1970s and 1980s—a full 36% (Murnane & Levy, 1993).

The neoconservative educational reform discourse and movement of the

1980s may be read as a rather direct response to economic restructuring, and as an attempt to bring curriculum and instruction in the nation's schools into closer alignment with new economic realities. The report of President Reagan's National Commission on Excellence in Education, *A Nation at Risk* (1983) was actually very postmodern in its assessment of the new "global village" created by informational technologies and multinational corporations and markets. It also recognized that "knowledge, learning, information, and skilled intelligence are the new raw materials of international commerce. . . . Learning is the indispensable investment required for success in the 'information age' we are entering" (pp. 6–7). Yet, neoconservatives also accepted rather than challenged the growing division of the economy into two major tiers of workers, each with different knowledge, learning, and information needs. Throughout the 1980s, the curriculum for students not bound for college (including many racial minorities and working-class students) was reconstructed around those "basic skills" or "functional literacy" skills deemed necessary for the new lower-tier jobs. Students demonstrated mastery of these skills by passing proficiency tests pegged to an eighth- or ninth-grade achievement level (Carlson, 1992). For college-bound students expected to enter the new high-skill, high tech labor force, neoconservative reform discourse emphasized the "new basics" of more math, science, and computer technology courses. Vocational education programs designed to prepare students for disappearing industrial or high-skill manual jobs, were eliminated or dramatically cut back (Gray, 1991).

While the neoconservative reform discourse accepted and even promoted the growing division of the labor force into two major tiers, neoliberal reform discourse has placed an emphasis on using the nation's schools to build a new "world-class" labor force that can compete for high-skill, high-wage jobs on the world market (Thurow, 1992). This has translated into support for a curriculum that emphasizes higher-order thinking skills for all students, including "constructivist" and inquiry approaches to math and science. It also has meant support for enrolling many more minority students and girls in math, science, and college preparatory courses. For those students not bound for 4-year colleges and universities, neoliberal discourse generally has endorsed what often is called "tech prep." This entails a strong emphasis on "workplace literacy" and "applied academics" in the last 2 years of high school, linked to the study of one of several occupational "clusters." Students then move onto more technical occupational training in 2-year programs at local community or technical colleges. Tech prep programs are designed to orient students toward "the middle range of occupations that require some postsecondary education and training, but not necessarily a baccalaureate degree" (Parnell, 1992, p. 25). These include the "paraprofessional" fields of nursing, computer processing, law enforcement, and office-machine maintenance, along with paralegals, engineering technicians, and banking and insurance. Neoliberals, then, have sought to reduce the emphasis on functional literacy and basic skills in urban schools and orient more general track students toward postsecondary education tied to a middle range of jobs.

Neoliberal reform discourse is democratic to the extent that it does not accept a two-tiered, highly inequitable society as our necessary or inevitable lot. It emphasizes the creation of quality jobs for all Americans and a curriculum that sets higher expectations for all students. The contradiction is that neoliberals to this point have not provided a sufficient mechanism or policy for restructuring the economy around high-quality jobs or for overcoming the dependence of the new postindustrial, information age on a large, relatively low-paid sector of service workers. Thus, the new occupational education programs, such as tech prep, may not be able to enroll many students since they are based on preparing young people for a middle range of jobs that continues to disappear. Schools can play their part in a national policy aimed at educating highly skilled workers, but the business community, as part of a national economic redevelopment policy, has to assume its share of the responsibility as well—to create high-quality jobs for all Americans at a decent wage. This suggests once more that a democratic progressive agenda for change in the postmodern era cannot continue to isolate and artificially separate educational renewal from a broader agenda for restructuring work in America.

OF "NORMALIZING" AND "POSTNORMALIZING" EDUCATIONAL REFORM

Foucault advanced the notion that a central or defining feature of the modernist era was a concern with what he called "normalization," a term that takes on a number of related meanings in Foucault's work. In one sense, it refers to a discourse and practice, within modern public institutions, that separate the "normal" from the "abnormal" and that bring the latter under the "gaze" of power. Prisons, along with mental institutions and arguably schools, are designed to normalize individuals in this sense. Foucault generally associated the normal with a subjectivity, or self, that is socialized and disciplined in such a way that it becomes more instrumental, that is, more economically productive and socially conforming. At other times, he clearly viewed the normal as a gendered and sexual category. In this sense, dominant identity groups (white, male, middle class, heterosexual, etc.) construct a discourse and practice in which they are viewed as normal, and members of nondominant identity groups are positioned as abnormal and therefore as deficient or lacking in one thing or another—as weak, sinful, unclean, lazy, unintelligent, diseased, or mentally ill. Since Foucault understood identity as a relational production, he emphasized that practices of normalization operate through a binary opposition that constructs both the normal and the abnormal, the Same and the Other, at one and the same time. This analysis of normalization obviously emphasizes the extent to which normalization serves to construct and legitimate oppressive power relations; and this is where Foucault's work challenges modernist claims regarding social progress through science. He links modernization to the "insidious extension" and further refinement of techniques of power and to the construction of docile subjectivities and bodies. He identifies as primary agents of this project both the powerful new state and the cadre of professional, scientific experts who take on the task of developing ever more effective techniques of normalization.

Foucault helps us understand a number of educational reform movements in this century as implicated in normalizing practices, but I want to limit my comments here to his discussion of the *examination* as one of the primary instruments of disciplinary power. Foucault's approach was to view the examination not only as a test of official knowledge, but also (and perhaps more important) as a ritual of power. He wrote: "It is a normalizing gaze, a surveillance that makes it possible to qualify, to classify and to punish. It establishes over individuals a visibility through which one differentiates them and judges them. . . . In it are combined the ceremony of power . . . and the establishment of truth" (Foucault, 1979, p. 184). This certainly helps explain the obsession with standardized testing in public education in this century. The standardized test and the testing situation embody the power of the institution and the state over the student and his or her future. Testing also is used to establish norms of achievement and intelligence against which all students are compared and some are found lacking. Those who do not measure up to the norm are likely to be assigned to low-ability groups and classes, where their identity as "slow" or "problem" learners is established and where they are likely to be treated as immature and thus in need of close supervision and discipline. Not coincidentally, class, gender, and race Others are most likely to be evaluated as deficient through this examination ritual.

Is any of this changing as we enter a postmodern historical era? Since Foucault was primarily a genealogist of the modern era, he did not have much to say about contemporary trends in normalization. Nevertheless, some of Foucault's later writings do begin to touch on this issue. For example, in an essay entitled "The Subject and Power" (1982), Foucault argued that at the current historical juncture, normalizing techniques of power are becoming both more individual and more totalizing. He suggested that the growing power of the state over individuals is based on a reappropriation of an old normalizing technique that originated in Christian institutions in the Middle Ages—which he called "pastoral power." Unlike the formal and legal power of the state over the individual that tended to predominate in the modern era, pastoral power cannot be exercised "without knowing the inside of people's minds, without exploring their souls, without making them reveal their innermost secrets. It implies a knowledge of the conscience and an ability to direct it'' (p. 214). As such, pastoral power is continuous for life and concerns itself with the "whole" self. Foucault found pastoral power operating in the renewed emphasis on personal relationships with clients in the medical and human services professions, in which clients are expected to produce detailed life histories, engage in confessional narratives about their problems, and schedule regular visits and checkups. The postmodern subject is thus ensnared, according to Foucault, in an ever-tighter web of regulatory and normalizing power.

There are indeed signs that normalizing regimes in public education are becoming more pastoral, individualizing, and totalizing in some of these ways. In fact, some of the more liberal, humanistic approaches to reform may be the most normalizing—at least potentially. The movement toward "authentic" or portfolio forms of assessment of students (and of student teachers) provides a case in point. Portfolio assessment generally is supported by progressive educators as an alternative to the standardized examination and as consistent with the personalization of instruction. It is based on the idea that everything students produce in the way of homework assignments, essays, autobiographical narratives, and tests is collected over the course of a year (or several years) for periodic review by teachers. When properly institutionalized, portfolio assessment provides a way of encouraging students to reflect on their learning and to decide what directions their learning should take next. However, when portfolio assessment is institutionalized within a normalizing discourse, these potentials are not likely to be realized. Instead, two effects seem likely. First, guidelines will be established that dictate what a "good" portfolio should look like, what constitutes an acceptable essay paper, and so on. In one large urban high school I am studying, teachers are given checklists for evaluating student portfolios; these checklists identify specific skills that are tested on the state's high school proficiency exam. In this form, portfolio assessment is certainly normalizing. Second, portfolios provide the possibility of extending evaluation in a pastoral way to include the "whole" student. In teacher education, for example, student teachers routinely are asked to keep portfolios that document their day-to-day teaching life, including journal entries of their thoughts about how well they are doing, their fears, their failures, and so forth. The portfolio in this case *may* become a confessional text to be read and evaluated by the student teacher's supervisor for signs of psychological imbalance, inappropriate attitudes, and lack of conformity to role expectations. In this form, journals and portfolios provide a more totalizing form of evaluation of the student teaching experience, which goes beyond classroom effectiveness to probe into personal motivations and psychological "adjustment."

These elements of individualizing, totalizing, and pastoral power also may be found in newer approaches to meeting the needs of special education students—that large and growing segment of the student population officially categorized as having learning disorders of one sort or another, being "emotionally disturbed," or being "socially maladjusted." Since passage of PL 94–142 in the 1970s, each special education student has been required to have an "individualized education plan" (IEP) that defines his or her educational problems and provides a plan for remediation that all involved parties, including parents, counselors, teachers, administrators, and human services professionals, have to sign off on. Now the model of the IEP is being advanced as a way of responding to the needs of other "at-risk" students, such as those who do not pass one or more sections of state-mandated proficiency tests. All of this, of course, is presented in very humanistic terms; and it is true that some young people have learning problems that demand our special attention. Nevertheless, the effect may be to bring various subpopulations of "abnormal" students under the more complete and total gaze of power with the objective of controlling them more efficiently and effectively.

Foucault (1982) argued that democratic projects could best be advanced within the current situation not through new state initiatives or work by progressive groups within the state, but rather through individual and collective "refusals" of the power of state agencies to normalize us. His image of a postmodern democratic society is one in which there is a continuous bringing into question of power relations and a continuous subversion, resistance, and demystification of power. As examples of such resistance or "anti-authority struggles," he cited a series of refusals or oppositions that have emerged in recent years, including "opposition to the power of men over women, of parents over children, of psychiatry over the mentally ill, of medicine over the population, of administration over the ways people live" (p. 211). According to Foucault, people also are challenging the linkage of power to qualifications, certification, and "expert" knowledge, and beginning to resist the secrecy of knowledge within the state and its agencies. These oppositions represent a refusal of state policies "which ignore who we are individually, and also a refusal of a scientific or administrative inquisition which determines who one is" (p. 212). When applied to public education this suggests, for example, the mobilization of resistance among teachers, students, and parents to labeling and categorizing practices that treat some young people as deficient or as not measuring up to a standardized norm. We sometimes forget the power of individual and collective resistance to power; Foucault reminds us that it has its place in making democratic progress. As recently as the late 1960s and early 1970s, resistance by students and their parents to dress codes designed to produce conforming student bodies proved to be quite effective in overturning many school dress codes as infringements on freedom of expression. Still there are limits to any politics grounded primarily in resistance to power and anti-statism. The real challenge in the years ahead, it seems to me, will be to develop a proactive agenda for change that includes struggle within the state to advance democratic educational policy.

PROGRESSIVE EDUCATIONAL REFORM IN THE POSTMODERN ERA

As we near the end of this century, a deepening cynicism has set in regarding the progressive project and the idea of progress. Many of those marginalized by class, race, gender, and sexual identity—for whom progressivism has promised equity—have become increasingly disillusioned with this promise and view it as bankrupt. Even the gains of the civil rights movement of the 1960s are being called into question, and with good cause. Over the past several decades many of the gains hard fought for have been rolled back, and legalistic remedies have failed to uproot deep-seated inequities in culture and everyday institutional life. In the academy, many critical theorists also have lost faith in progress. Melucci (1989a) goes so far as to assert that we have become "nomads of the present," and that democratic projects must be understood in terms of making pragmatic gains in the here-and-now for the particular social movements with which we identify. I have sought in this chapter to recognize the importance of this questioning of progress and progressivism that is going on in American culture and in critical educational studies, without abandoning the progressive project. The idea of progress needs to be reconceptualized consistent with postmodern insights, and progressivism needs to be reconfigured if it is to play a viable role in leading public education into the next century. Belief in the possibility of progress toward a "good society"—one that is more equitable, in which individuals and groups have greater freedom to control their lives and explore their full potentials, and in which the self is constructed within the context of a caring, mutually supportive community—may be essential to the furtherance of democratic projects. I think the three strands of postmodern theorizing I have examined above provide useful interpretive frames for rethinking progress in education in the postmodern era, although they certainly are not alone in this regard. One of the defining features of postmodernism is a movement away from unifying meta-narratives toward the interweaving of diverse theoretical strands that lead in a number of different directions.

It is also clear that democratic progressivism in education will have to live with certain tensions, ambiguities, and contradictions that may not be fully resolvable. Foremost among these is the tension between representing "community" or "public" interests and representing "special" interests. We must find a way of celebrating cultural diversity that does not feed into a further erosion of community. The challenge is to reconstruct a democratic, multicultural community, with public education playing a leading role in that process; but balancing the claims of diversity and community will not be easy. Related to this is a tension concerning the relative influence of various axes of cultural struggle and identity in shaping progressive discourse. Postmodernism is associated with a movement beyond class reductionistic and deterministic models of education and culture. Yet it does not follow that all progressive struggles are of equal significance in defining a given situation or in challenging given structures of domination. It is clear that economic forces and class struggles are deeply implicated in the construction of inequality. At the same time, struggles organized around gender, race, and sexuality are also central to understanding current cultural dynamics and can no longer be viewed as of peripheral or subsidiary importance compared with class dynamics. A final tension in postmodern progressivism has to do with using state power to advance democratic projects without promoting a concentration of power in the state or an expansion of bureaucratic state apparatuses and regulatory constraints that limit individual freedom and local, democratic control of public schools. Because of these tensions, a democratic progressive discourse in education must always be in the process of being "made" through an inclusive dialogue on the meaning of progress.

3

Making Tracks

The "Detracking" and Retracking of Public Education

THE PARTICULAR CHARACTER of the public high school in the United States was stamped on it by "The Cardinal Principles of Secondary Education," an influential commission report published by the National Education Association (1918). That report called for the establishment of a "comprehensive" high school, by which it meant a high school that mixed students of all socioeconomic backgrounds, abilities, and aspirations, providing a diversity of course offerings and curricular programs to meet the needs of all. The comprehensive high school as defined and characterized in the Cardinal Principles was—at least on paper—a very democratic institution. Whether students were preparing for college and the professions or were enrolled in vocational programs, they were made part of the "embryonic community" of the school. Students came together across their differences in "core" classes and in extracurricular activities. This was a school that seemed explicitly designed to build a more democratic community, one in which difference was recognized and allowed for, but in which explicit efforts were made to build bonds of community and common interest (Lazerson, 1991). It is thus, I would like to suggest, a vision of secondary education that is very much attuned to democratic progressivism in the postmodern era. In a sense, I want to argue, what we need to do is reappropriate the democratic vision of the comprehensive high school, with modifications, but this time ensure that it is realized in practice.

Beyond the democratic veneer of the comprehensive high school, as Joel Spring (1989) has observed, has stood the image of the "sorting machine," an institution heavily involved in sorting students for unequal educations and channeling them toward highly unequitable futures. These sorting practices typically are referred to as "tracking," although no high school in the United States actually admits to having "tracks," since that term tends to have a negative connotation. High schools often go out of their way to hide tracking practices, so that even students sometimes have little idea that they are in a track and less idea of how they got into it. School officials will admit that they have different calibers of academic courses—some for those planning to pursue college and

40

general academic courses that, while technically acceptable for college admission, typically are not viewed as college preparatory by college admissions officers. Aside from these differentiated academic courses, most high schools have several vocational program offerings, which students often take at a separate vocational-technical campus. These tracking practices not only play a major part in channeling students toward unequal futures; they also play a part in reproducing class, race, and gender inequality from one generation to the next. That is, tracking practices have had the effect (and sometimes the intent) of separating white from Black students, middle-class from poor students, and girls from boys in ways that advantage the former and disadvantage the latter. This occurs for a number of reasons having to do with expectations on the part of students, parents, guidance counselors, teachers, and others, along with the discriminating impact of standardized testing. Finally, the effect of both the production of inequality and the reproduction of inequality through tracking practices has been to subvert the idea of the school as an embryonic democratic community. "School spirit," organized around interscholastic athletic competition, has served as a pale and distorted substitute for community in the high school, and even this increasingly fails to provide a common ground.

Consequently, by the mid-1960s, the democratic ideal of the comprehensive high school as a site where students from diverse backgrounds could learn together and participate together in building a democratic civic life, had been seriously eroded. This erosion also was related to the segregation of American communities by class and race, and the growing divisions between conditions in urban centers, where poverty was on the rise, and the suburbs that had sprung up around these urban centers, where the white middle class was experiencing a steady rise in income. Tracking existed between schools as well as within schools. Students in urban and suburban high schools could almost be said to be in two different tracks—the former oriented toward high school graduation and the entry-level work force, and the latter oriented toward college and the professional-managerial work force.

Democratic progressives from John Dewey (1916) to Jeannie Oakes (1985) have decried tracking practices in public education. However, because tracking practices have been such persistent features of high school life in this century, and because public education has been so involved in the production of inequality, it will not be easy to "detrack" the nation's schools. Yet, suddenly it seems that that is exactly what is happening, or at least what is being called for by major actors involved in the formulation of educational policy. Almost everyone is jumping on the detracking bandwagon, including groups such as the National Governors' Conference and the Carnegie Foundation—among the most influential power brokers in shaping state educational policy in recent years (Brewer, Rees, & Argys, 1995; Mansnerus, 1992). Within recent reform discourse, detracking at the high school level has been associated with two major reforms.

First, detracking has been used to refer to the closing of many or most vocational programs in neighborhood high schools and the closer integration of remaining vocational students with ''regular'' students in the general academic track. Second, detracking has been used to refer to a shift from the ability grouping of students to heterogeneous grouping, with students advancing through the curriculum at their own pace.

On the surface at least, these reforms, if hardly transformative, seem worthy of support and potentially consistent with democratic progressive values. However, as I will argue in this chapter, detracking reforms actually are occurring within the context of a more significant and far-reaching retracking of high school students. Although I want to focus my comments on urban high schools, where tracking practices are most closely linked to the reproduction of class and race inequality, much of what I have to say applies to developments in smaller and rural communities as well. In laying out this discussion, I want to examine recent developments in each of the three traditional tracks in secondary education—the general academic, vocational, and college preparatory tracks. I will relate recent shifts in tracking practices to shifts occurring in education and culture in the late twentieth century. Some of these changes are economic in origin, while others have to do with the mounting fiscal crisis of the state, while still others are related to the breakdown of traditional conceptions of community in the United States. I will conclude with some thoughts on the formulation of a democratic progressive discourse on the detracking of public schools.

BUILDING THE NEW BASIC SKILLS TRACK

A good place to begin a discussion of the retracking of secondary education in the United States is with a look at changes in enrollments in various tracks. An examination of data from the U.S. Department of Education reveals that in the decade between 1982 and 1992, some quite dramatic shifts were taking place in tracking practices. The general academic track, which leads most directly to the entry-level, high school graduate labor force, grew very rapidly, from about 35% of high school seniors to over 45%. This rise was even more dramatic, from 40% to 56%, for the lowest socioeconomic quartile of students—most of whom attend inner-city or rural schools. Meanwhile the proportion of students enrolled in college preparatory courses grew at a moderate pace, from 38% of all seniors to 43%. Enrollment of students from the lowest socioeconomic quartile in college preparatory courses remained virtually stagnant over the decade, rising only slightly from 21% to 23%. Finally, the big loser among the high school tracks was vocational education. Enrollment plummeted over the decade from 27% to 12%. For the poorest students, enrollment in vocational programs fell from about 40% to slightly over 20%. Over the course of only 10 years, vocational enrollments fell by more than 50% in most districts (U.S. Department of Education, National Center for Education Statistics, 1995, Table 134).

In attempting to make sense of these changes, I want to begin with a discussion of changes in the general academic track, the growth of which has been the most dramatic. One of the most obvious reasons why this track has grown so rapidly, even though it has been much criticized for lowering academic standards and providing students with a "watered down" curriculum that prepares them for little after high school, is that the job market for high school graduates keeps growing. Between 1990 and 2005, the service sector of the economy is expected to contribute approximately 50% of all new jobs to the U.S. labor force. By comparison, it contributed about 43% of all new jobs from 1975 to 1990 (Kutscher, 1992). In sheer numbers, the largest subdivisions of the service sector are those in which skill requirements and wages are relatively low, employment is often part-time, and there are few or no health benefits. These include jobs such as waiters, household workers, janitors and maintenance workers, security guards, and food-service workers, along with jobs involving routine data entry and processing on computer terminals. It is estimated that only about one-half of all service industry jobs pay more than the minimum wage (Johnson, 1993). The rapid growth of the general academic track is thus very closely linked to the growth of this new service sector work force.

In fact, reform discourse over the past decade or so oriented toward the general academic track has been organized quite explicitly around the theme of improving the "functional literacy" skills of entry-level workers and thus increasing the nation's economic competitiveness. As a result, the general academic track curriculum has been radically reconstituted. Where once courses offered a watered down version of the college preparatory curriculum, by the mid-1980s the curriculum was about teaching students a core set of "basic skills" and testing them to see that they were proficient in these skills before they graduated. According to the National Commission on Excellence in Education (1983), basic skills were the skills individuals needed "to secure gainful employment, and to manage their own lives" (p. 8). Functional literacy skills usually were associated with an eighth- or ninth-grade achievement level, the level at which most state proficiency tests for high school graduation were set.

Although basic skills reform discourse generally has not differentiated between schools and school districts, it is clear that its impact has been felt most in urban districts. It is in urban districts where the majority of students traditionally have been oriented toward the high school graduate work force and where the language and culture represented in standardized tests are most alien. Of course, basic literacy skills in English are essential for young people if they hope to advance themselves; but because functional literacy skills have been set at such a low level and linked to the needs of entry-level, low-wage workers, they have not been consistent with the development of critical literacy or the kinds of higher-order thinking skills valued in higher-tier jobs. Nor have they provided room for students to affirm their own cultural and linguistic backgrounds. As a result, a basic skills curriculum has not helped empower most urban students. Expectations are lowered to basic skills mastery and high school graduation, all in the name of raising standards and holding students accountable. In the meantime, the "drill-'em-and-test-'em" routine has been associated with a very high dropout rate, so that only about half of all inner-city ninth graders stay in the system long enough to graduate (Carlson, 1989).

In the 1990s, the basic skills reform discourse increasingly has moved beyond a concern with language and math skills and begun to define functional literacy more broadly. One area of functional literacy that is gaining much more attention is what often is called "technological literacy." Unfortunately, the kind of technological literacy that has been emphasized in basic skills reform discourse is very similar to that emphasized in lower-tier jobs. So far, we lack detailed empirical studies on how students are using computers in basic skills classrooms. My own observations and work with students in urban high schools suggest that computers most often are used in one of several ways. Students often play interactive "skill-building" games on computers that teach them basic skills within the context of a graphic game for either one or two students. Usually students are rewarded with this activity after they have completed their regular assigned work. Students also are assigned to computers for individualized remedial instruction, sometimes in special remedial education computer labs. Finally, students often use word processing programs to complete comprehension-level questions about a text they have been reading. Seymour Papert (1993), one of the pioneers in the use of computers in education, refers to these as "tightly" programmed usages, with the programmer "cast in the role of a 'knowledge architect' who will specify a plan, a tight program, for the placement of 'knowledge bricks' in children's minds" (p. 207).

Also receiving increasing attention in the 1990s as part of the new basic skills are interpersonal skills related to being a good "team player" and learning how to cooperate with others in accomplishing work tasks (Pullin, 1994; Secretary's Commission on Achieving Necessary Skills, 1991). All of this is very much in tune with the new management discourse in business and reflects shifts in the organization of work in a postindustrial economy. The so-called "new paradigm" in management theory has begun to have an impact on educational reform discourse in recent years in some important ways. For example, William Spady (1992), who developed outcome-based learning, talks of a shift in educational reform from seeing "students as isolated performers" to seeing "students as collaborative performers." He observes: "What some call 'Getting along' and 'Working together for the common good' . . . have within the past decade become issues of urgency within the world of work" (p. 22). Spady maintains that states and school districts should establish outcome goals for students that have to do with demonstrating effectiveness as team members who "can successfully contribute their best efforts to achieve success in collaborative endeavors" (p. 58). Certainly, cooperative learning skills, competencies, or virtues need to be developed within democratic cultures. However, when these concepts and approaches to educational reform are embedded within an economic rather than a democratic discourse—one that emphasizes adjusting or "normalizing" young people to the world of work and socializing them to docility—then cooperative learning is more disempowering than empowering.

I have suggested to this point that the growth of the new basic skills track is related to the growth of a new service sector economy and the presumed skill needs of entry-level workers. Economic elites not only have promoted an economic rationale for curriculum reform. At the same time, they have promoted cost-effective models of organizing instruction and public schools, that is, ones that improve performance and reduce costs at the same time. This concern with cost-effective models of instruction has heightened in a time of fiscal cutbacks in the state, and basic skills models of instruction are at least partially a response to this concern. This is based on the rationale that student achievement levels on standardized tests can be raised and costs lowered by spending more "time on task" with basic skills and eliminating almost everything else. A good example of this rationale is provided by the recent report of the National Education Commission on Time and Learning (NECTL), *Prisoners of Time* (1994). The NECTL was established by Congress as an advisory body. Its nine-member board, selected by Congress and the Department of Education, reads like a "who's who" of power brokers in public school policy, including members representing the conservative think tank (the Hudson Institute) and the major corporate player in education (the Business Roundtable). The report bemoans the fact that schools are burdened with "a whole set of requirements for what has been called 'the new work of the schools'—education about personal safety, consumer affairs, AIDS, conservation and energy, family life, driver's training—as well as traditional nonacademic activities, such as counseling, gym, study halls, homeroom, lunch and pep rallies" (p. 10). If these are to be made available to students, according to the report, they should be offered after the regular school day so that during the regular school day the focus can be kept on mastery of basic skills. The report notes:

> Establishing an academic day means, in essence, that the existing school day be devoted almost exclusively to core academic instruction. What this means is obvious: many worthwhile student programs—athletics, clubs, and other activities—will have to be sacrificed unless the school day is lengthened. (p. 32)

This can be taken two ways. On the most literal level, the report is recommending the lengthening of the school day so that these "worthwhile" activities can

be maintained. However, it is also suggesting that if the school day is not length-
ened, those activities not narrowly linked to basic skills mastery in the core
subject areas will have to go. In most urban districts lengthening the school day
is not a very realistic option financially or otherwise. The implications in this
case are, I think, alarming. The report in effect provides a rationale for further
cuts in program offerings and staff (such as counselors; music, art, and physical
education teachers; and librarians). It is also distressing, I think, that the report
lumps together consumer affairs, AIDS education, and conservation education
in the same category with driver's training—as subjects that "steal" from time
spent on basic skills. Thus the report also provides a rationale for eliminating
the last vestiges of a progressive, student-centered curriculum within the new
basic skills track—all in the name of raising test scores and lowering costs.

The growth of a basic skills curriculum in the general academic track may
be related to another element of cost-effectiveness—cutting labor costs. A basic
skills curriculum can be programmed to make it self-paced, and by bringing
more computers into basic skills classes, fewer teachers may be needed. Such is
the hope expressed in a report by the conservative Brookings Institution, *Making
Schools Work* (Hanushek, 1994). The report speaks of the "advantages to using
certain kinds of technology for instructional purposes—including drill and practice activities on computers." Among the major advantages, according to the
report, would be "the substitution of capital [i.e., technology] for labor in
schools," an advantage that the report fears teachers will resist without the right
mix of incentives, since "they are unlikely to advocate the adoption of technologies that will . . . threaten them as a group with decreased employment possibilities" (p. 78). We are likely to hear more in the years ahead about bringing
computers into the classroom to replace teachers and thereby reduce the single
largest cost in public education as in industry—that of labor. This also suggests
that a battle may be looming between teachers' unions and certain uses of computer technology in the classroom.

Ironically, all of these developments associated with the shift to a basic
skills curriculum, which are having a very damaging impact on urban schools
in particular, are being represented in the language of detracking and better
meeting the needs of students. Detracking in this case is associated with a movement away from homogeneous grouping of students in ability groups toward
the heterogeneous grouping of students working at their own pace, "mastering"
one skill at a time. According to the NECTL (1994), mastery learning "makes it
possible for today's schools to escape the assembly-line mentality of the 'factory
model' school. . . . Instead of the lock-step of lecture and laboratory, computers
and other new telecommunications make it possible for students to move at their
own pace" (p. 37). Heterogeneous grouping, in this case, is related to the *pacing* of a predetermined learning process rather than the *personalization* of the
learning process, which would be more progressive. It is a form of detracking

that replaces the assembly-line metaphor of instruction with one equally reductionistic and disempowering—that of computer-guided instruction. Unfortunately, this means that the movement to heterogeneous grouping of students is not necessarily progressive in the democratic sense. This also reminds us that slogans like "detracking" have no fixed or stable meaning, and that they can take on quite different meanings within the context of different reform discourses.

THE NEW VOCATIONALISM

I indicated earlier that one reason the general academic track has grown so rapidly in the past decade or so is that enrollments in vocational education programs have fallen off so rapidly. Nationally, the numbers enrolled in vocational education programs peaked in 1984. Then, in the decade between 1984 and 1994, enrollments began to fall off sharply (Gray, 1991). A number of prestigious foundations even began suggesting by the mid-1980s that vocational education be eliminated entirely (Claus, 1990). The collapse of vocational education in recent years may be attributed to a complex set of interrelated factors. One obvious problem was that in a de-industrializing economy, where the most substantial growth has been in the low-paying, low-skill service sector, vocational education programs have had an increasingly difficult time placing graduates in jobs they are trained for and at wages significantly above minimum wage. Most employers in the expanding service sector of the labor force prefer that their new workers have generalizable literacy and math skills rather than specialized, technical training, which is often too narrow and quickly outdated.

Other factors contributed to the decline of vocational education. For example, the vocational programs offered to students in the 1970s and 1980s in many cases continued to be linked to a gendered division of labor at a time when the women's movement was pushing schools to do more to promote gender equity and when adolescent girls where beginning to challenge traditional gender roles. From the 1920s through the 1970s, the vocational education programs with the largest enrollments were trade and industry programs designed to train boys in the use of heavy industrial equipment, and home economics programs designed to prepare girls to be "good" homemakers and mothers (U. S. Department of Education, National Center for Education Statistics, 1980, Table 144). With the passage of Title IX in the early 1970s, which outlawed discrimination in educational programs receiving federal funds, many vocational education programs were unable, or unwilling, to change rapidly enough. Moreover, vocational education suffered generally from an "image problem." Over the years it had developed an image as a track for "low-ability" or "low-achievement" students. This image or representation of vocational education not only kept many students away from vocational programs, but also provided a rationale for closing vocational programs, since policy makers could claim that by eliminating such programs they were promoting higher standards for students. Finally, budgetary considerations played a big part in the decline of vocational education in the 1980s. As student enrollment in vocational education dropped off sharply, already high per pupil costs skyrocketed, state funding of vocational education programs continued to decline, and local school officials found that shutting down vocational programs offered a "quick-fix" way to cut costs.

Kenneth Gray (1991), a leading scholar in the field of vocational education, has posed the question of whether vocationalism might, like the phoenix, rise from its own ashes in the years ahead. The jury is still out on that question, although there are indeed signs that vocational education is staging something of a comeback, often under a different name, such as occupational education. Behind these changes, however, there are continuities between the "old" and the "new" vocationalism—including a tendency among both to emphasize an overly conforming conception of work roles and an overly utilitarian conception of education. To the extent that the new vocationalism can be distinguished from the old, it is primarily because newer models call for a much closer integration of academic and applied occupational education, which blurs the distinction between the vocational track and the general academic track.

So far, the new vocationalism or occupational education is still in embryonic form, and a number of factors may limit its further development. However, there are clear signs of change. For one thing, students in the new occupational education programs typically take many of their classes with general academic track students and take occupationally related courses only as electives for several periods a day. This is a dramatic change from the completely separate courses that typically were offered to vocational and academic students in the past—along with completely separate sets of teachers on separate campuses. If advocates of the new vocationalism have their way—and they represent powerful interest groups in school reform—we are likely to see other changes, among them that general academic classes will become more occupationally oriented, thus completing the detracking of vocational and general academic track students. According to a report by the U.S. Department of Education entitled *Goals 2000: Building Bridges from School to Work* (1993), many communities are rethinking the practice of tracking and are eliminating or phasing out outdated vocational programs along with general track courses. It concludes that students in "general" programs "take a random selection of courses that lead nowhere, exiting high school with a diploma that is practically worthless" (p. 6). The report recommends that all or almost all general academic track students learn work skills and gain work experience, and suggests organizing core academic courses around occupational or work themes and linking students more closely with the "real" world of work outside the school.

Building Bridges endorses a variety of different types of occupational programs to achieve this end. Youth apprenticeships involve placing students in work sites for part of the school day under the supervision of skilled craftspeople, who teach students skills of the trade and serve as mentors. So far, however, very few students are involved in apprenticeship programs, largely because it is hard to find adequate placements and ensure that students are getting an education on the job and not just being exploited as cheap labor (Kantor, 1994). Another model endorsed in the report is "cooperative education." In these programs, students may spend mornings at school and afternoons working at a local business. According to the report about 8% of American eleventh and twelfth graders participate in cooperative learning programs. Unfortunately, one of the reasons for the relative success of cooperative education may be that such programs are less discriminating in finding placements for students, which also means that many students end up working in service industry sites, including those in the fast food industry. A third model of occupational education endorsed in the report is the "career academy." This, according to the report, is "a school within a larger school, where a group of students and a team of teachers stay together for a several-hour block of time each day. These students and teachers often remain together for three years. Instruction is focused on a single industry cluster" (p. 3). A final occupational education model endorsed by the report is "tech prep." Tech prep programs sometimes are called "2 + 2" programs because they involve 2 years of high school and 2 years of postsecondary instruction. For example, students may choose among several occupational clusters such as business/management, engineering/mechanical, and health/human services.

According to *Building Bridges*, a major theme in all of these occupational education programs is "business and industry sitting across from educators as *equal partners* at the table to work toward mutual goals" (p. 5). As one example of a possible partnership between public education and the business community, the report suggests making records on student performance available to prospective employers in a region through a computerized management information system (MIS). This will, according to the report, "send a clear message to students: That their school performance counts" (p. 8). Such systems also send a clear message that education is about job training and learning to be a "good worker" more than a critical citizen.

Reform discourse such as that represented by *Building Bridges* raises serious doubts about the capacity of a "new" vocational education to overcome the limitations of the "old" vocationalism. No matter how appealing its supporters make it sound in terms of motivating students and making learning more relevant to their "real life" needs, the new vocationalism continues to participate in the channeling of some students toward low-skill, low-wage jobs and sets very low expectations for these students. Programs such as tech prep, which supposedly are to prepare students for a "middle range" of jobs requiring some postsecondary education, must face the hard reality that this middle sector of the labor force has continued to shrink in proportion to the service sector (Grubb, 1992). Finally, the new vocationalism, like the new basic skills curriculum, continues to take for granted an economically functional model of education. John Dewey, in *Democracy and Education* (1916), warned of the dangers of this kind of economic functionalism in the discourse of vocational education. "There is," he wrote, "a danger that vocational education will be interpreted in theory and practice as trade education: as a means of securing technical efficiency in specialized future pursuits. Education would then become an instrument of perpetuating unchanged the existing industrial order of society, instead of operating as a means of its transformation" (p. 316). Certainly, work is a central life experience and as part of their schooling students should learn about work. Education in its most engaging and productive sense is a form of work experience. Nevertheless, the new vocationalism does not appear to provide a basis for empowering students, and it will likely continue to participate in the production and reproduction of class, race, and gender inequalities.

MAGNET SCHOOLS AND THE NEW COLLEGE PREPARATORY TRACK

As the general academic track and the new vocational education track are becoming more closely integrated, the college preparatory track is being more fully differentiated from these other, lower-tier tracks and spatially separated from them. This, in turn, may be related to the growth of a more two-tiered socioeconomic order, in which the new middle class has sought to distance itself—culturally and spatially—from the new working and underclasses. "Magnet" schools—specialized schools that draw students from throughout a district and have admission requirements—are enrolling an increasingly large proportion of college-bound students, particularly in urban school districts. As the college preparatory track is being relocated to magnet schools in these urban districts, the remaining "comprehensive" neighborhood high schools are not really comprehensive any more.

Curriculum reform within the new college preparatory track, as with the other tracks, has been based on an economic rationale, in this case involving the skill requirements for new high-wage, high-skill, high tech jobs. Whether it is designing a new product or the assembly line to produce it, or whether it is making decisions about how to meet customer needs or design commercial images to appeal to a new market niche, the new professional, managerial, and scientific jobs require much more than minimum basic skills. One of the most articulate statements of how the skill needs of the new college-educated labor force are changing is the report of the Carnegie Foundation for the Advancement of Teaching, *A Nation Prepared; Teachers for the Twenty-First Century* (1986). According to the report, the new high tech and professional-managerial jobs are dependent on people who "have a good intuitive grasp of the ways in which all kinds of physical and social systems work." They must "possess a feeling for mathematical concepts and the ways in which they can be applied to difficult problems, an ability to see patterns of meaning where others see only confusion, a cultivated creativity that leads them to new problems, new products, and new services before their competitors get to them" (p. 44).

This metaphor of the student as a knowledge-production worker has led to a growing interest in a "constructivist" curriculum in college preparatory classes. Constructivism as a movement and curriculum reform discourse has emerged out of the fields of science and mathematics education in recent years, although something very similar—what we might call social constructionism—is becoming influential in college preparatory English, social studies, and other classes. Constructivist approaches to curriculum and pedagogy are based on a nonreified conception of knowledge, that is, one that treats knowledge as something that is constructed by individuals and groups as they grapple to solve concrete problems in unique ways (Doll, 1994). The college preparatory curriculum, consequently, is becoming more progressive in ways that Dewey would have appreciated. Nevertheless, the limitations of constructivism as a reform discourse and practice are considerable as well, at least from a democratic progressive standpoint. Foremost among these is the fact that constructivism has been linked primarily to an economic rationale in state reform discourse. As with basic skills and occupational education reform discourse, within constructivist discourse curriculum decisions are reduced to questions about how we prepare young people to be "better" (i.e., more productive) workers rather than how we should prepare young people for participation in the reconstruction of a democratic culture and community life. Furthermore, as the general academic curriculum has been reorganized around routine "basic skills," the gulf between the curriculum and pedagogy of the general track and the increasingly constructivist curriculum and pedagogy of the college preparatory track is becoming more difficult to bridge.

The gulf developing between the general and college preparatory tracks in expectations for students, curriculum, and pedagogy is facilitating and perhaps even encouraging the spatial separation of the two tracks. Many college preparatory students are enrolled in magnet schools or school-within-a-school programs. Such schools and programs are open to students from throughout a district or a high school attendance area, typically have some admission requirements, and often organize instruction around themes or specialized programs (e.g., performing arts, math-science, communications, the humanities, etc.) (Metz, 1988; Young & Clinchy, 1992). They typically are free from many central office and state regulations pertaining to class schedules, course offerings, and student evaluation, and may be given greater control over hiring of teachers and administrators so that they can attract and retain a qualified, committed staff. Not everyone who attends a magnet school is college bound; and at this point the majority of college-bound students are being educated in neighborhood high schools. Still, the trend, at least in urban districts, is toward the greater separation of the college track from neighborhood high schools and its relocation in magnet schools.

The emergence of magnet schools over the past decade in urban districts also may be interpreted as an attempt by dominant power brokers in public education to maintain adequate funding for quality college preparatory programs in a system that is otherwise being fiscally starved. As budgets have been slashed, magnet schools have continued to flourish. According to one study, school districts spend on the average 10–12% more per pupil to operate magnet schools and programs; a recent study of magnet schools in St. Louis found that the district spent 25–42% more on magnet students than on nonmagnet students (Young & Clinchy, 1992). Aside from receiving more aid from the school district, magnet schools and programs are much more likely to be linked with corporate and foundation "partners" that provide further financial support. Magnet schools, then, often are allowed to become "investment sites" for outside capital, unlike "regular" neighborhood schools. For example, the RJR Nabisco Foundation's "Next Century Schools Program" allocates large grants to individual magnet schools rather than to school districts (Jehl & Payzant, 1992). Corporations and business foundations support magnet schools because this allows them to focus their philanthropic efforts on one or several schools, where it is possible to see results. These changes raise disturbing prospects of a two-tiered system of public education, one (for those bound for college and middle-class jobs) well financed with the help of corporate capital, and one (for those bound for the new working and underclasses) fiscally starved. All of this threatens to override efforts by state supreme courts to equalize per pupil spending.

Ironically, magnet schools also have important democratic potential and often have been supported by democratic progressives. They were developed originally in the 1970s and 1980s in response to court-ordered desegregation of major northern school districts, since they provided an appealing way of promoting school desegregation without an overreliance on compulsory school assignments and busing (Metz, 1986). The rationale has been that spaces in magnet schools can be filled to maintain a racial composition very similar to the composition of students in the district as a whole. In order to encourage enough white parents and students to consider enrolling in magnet schools, they offer top-quality education. However, because of their limited number, magnet schools have not replaced busing to achieve racial balance as much as they have supplemented it. Timothy Young and Evans Clinchy (1992) note that there has been "no instance where a major school system has achieved noticeable desegregation in its public schools by using a voluntary magnet program" (p. 24). At the same time, there is abundant evidence that indicates that magnet schools have contributed to class segregation, something the courts and school districts did not recognize (or care to recognize) in their narrow focus on achieving racial balance. According to Mary Metz (1988), author of one of the most influential studies of magnet schools in the 1980s, "Magnet schools are often designed for students who achieve best and are organized around curricular emphases more likely to appeal to elites than to a cross section of citizens. In many communities, all or most magnets developed are schools for the gifted and talented, or high schools stressing math and science, or at best schools for the performing arts" (p. 57). Metz notes the irony in school policy that declares all schools officially equal, "even as middle-class parents and alert working-class parents diligently strive to place their children in schools where the education will be more than equal . . . [and] where merit is far more likely to blossom" (pp. 58–59).

Magnet schools, for all of their faults and elitist tendencies, have in some instances provided space for groups of teachers along with progressive groups in the community to "reinvent" education in democratic ways. For example, although they are the exception rather than the rule, some magnet schools have sought explicitly to serve low-income students, have an open admissions policy, and are governed by boards composed of teachers, students, and community groups. Magnet schools are also worth supporting in principle at least, because they provide students and parents with some choice over students' education. While choice in education most often has been associated with conservative voucher plans to privatize public education, choice is also a basic democratic value. Finally, because students have to apply to be admitted to magnet schools and typically go through some admission process, they are likely to be more committed to the school and to their own education—something so often lacking when students are assigned to a school and told what to learn. Thus the magnet school movement at this point in time is deeply contradictory, and democratic educational policy will need to carve out a middle ground, seeking to maintain the desirable features of magnet schools while working to overcome their current limitations.

The recent expansion of magnet schools in the New York City school system provides a good case study of the contradictory character of the magnet school movement in the mid-1990s. Between 1993 and 1995, the New York City school system established 48 experimental magnet high schools, 46 of them schools with enrollments of 110 to 600 students. The new magnet schools were started by an unlikely coalition of very diverse groups under the banner of the Network for School Renewal, including the Fund for New York City Public Education (a private philanthropic group that channels corporate funds to public schools), the Center for Collaborative Education (an umbrella urban reform coalition affiliated with the Coalition of Essential Schools), the Manhattan Institute (a conservative research group that supports school choice plans), Acorn (a community organization of low-income residents), and the Annenberg Foundation (a corporate foundation). The latter group donated $25 million to the project and has agreed to support an additional 50 small magnet high schools by the year 2000 (Dillon & Berger, 1995; Henderson & Raywid, 1994). By that time magnet schools in the city are expected to serve about 50,000 students, or approximately 5% of the city's projected 1.3 million students (Dillon & Berger, 1995). While this may still be a relatively small proportion of the total, if current growth rates were to continue over the next decade or two, magnet schools could enroll a substantial proportion of students in the system. In order to allow magnet schools to innovate and provide top-quality education, the coalition is attempting to gain special status for the schools as a type of "educational free-trade zone," known formally as a "learning zone," that is unencumbered by bureaucratic regulations and red tape (Dillon, 1995).

A special *New York Times* series on the new magnet schools in 1995 was full of praise for the constructivist, student-centered learning going on in the schools. According to one article,

> Within many schools, there has been a radical break with the traditional disciplines. . . . In a course whose theme is water, classes may be taught some biology as they study fish, chemistry as they look at river pollution and a smattering of physics as they examine ocean currents. . . . Many experimental school directors criticize traditional tests. Students at only 13 of the 30 new high schools . . . took even one state Regents test in 1993–1994. (Dillon & Berger, 1995, p. B11)

Another article in the series featured a magnet school named the El Puente Academy for Peace and Justice, which trains young people on Williamsburg's predominantly Hispanic south side to become community activists. On a typical day at the school, the article noted,

> Jennifer [a student] was documenting traffic flow for a 10th grade science lesson on how pollution affects the respiratory system. Marilyn and her friends in the ninth grade surveyed neighborhood advertising, the first step in a lobbying campaign against local merchants to reduce the barrage of cigarette and beer ads. Nytopia was helping build a community garden. . . . A discussion about environmental racism . . . arose out of the area's coexistence with several waste-collection businesses, legal and illegal, and its designation as the proposed site for an incinerator. (Gonzalez, 1995, pp. A1, A14)

Yet another article featured a school named Renaissance, run entirely by teachers. It observed, "Teachers in Renaissance do not have to use ancient textbooks and rigid school-wide lesson plans; they can pick and choose from a variety of texts, workbooks, novels, and newspapers, or write their own curriculum" (Firestone, 1995, p. A12).

These would appear to be promising sites for the reinvention of the public high school in ways that effectively empower teachers, students, and progressive community groups, and relate education to students' real-life concerns and interests. As I noted earlier, however, the fact that magnet schools are in most cases privileged educational sites for college preparatory students places severe restrictions on their current democratic potential. It will be hard to challenge this privilege, for part of what currently gives magnet schools their identity and appeal among the middle class is this privilege. The high expectations set for magnet school students are the opposite side of the coin of the low expectations set for general track students in neighborhood high schools. The high per pupil costs in magnet schools are offset by low per pupil costs in other schools. As long as magnet schools are constructed within the context of such bipolar oppositions and participate in tracking practices, they hardly seem worthy of support. The challenge is thus to reconstruct the idea of specialized, small schools within the context of a more democratic discourse and practice.

BEYOND THE DILEMMAS OF DETRACKING AND RETRACKING

While the developments I have explored are complex and dynamic, one thing is clear: Curricular tracks are not disappearing in public high schools, despite all the talk of detracking. Tracks also are still very much implicated in the production and reproduction of inequality. How should democratic forces respond to these developments? Let me say at the outset that there are no easy answers to this question, in that all responses involve dilemmas and tensions. For example, it is not even clear whether the proper response to problems associated with tracking should be "detracking." To the extent that the term *tracking* is used to refer to the current system of curriculum differentiation, which channels students toward highly inequitable futures, democratic progressives should oppose tracking. However, to the extent that tracking implies curriculum differentiation, greater choice for students and parents, and moving beyond a "one size fits all" curriculum, then detracking is not necessarily an unbridled good. Detracking may even be associated with some reform discourses that need to be opposed, such as the reconstitution of the general academic curriculum around a highly fragmented and prepackaged set of skills to be mastered.

Perhaps the most pragmatic and practical response might be to attempt to make current tracking practices a bit less discriminatory. Reba Page, in her study *Lower-Track Classrooms* (1991), suggests that to help counter the tendency of a differentiated curriculum to track students according to class, gender, and race, placement decisions should be continually revisited and reviewed. Beyond that, we also might seek to make each of the existing tracks in secondary education less unequal in terms of financial resources and (more important) the kinds of educational experiences to which students are exposed. All young people have a right to a curriculum that develops their critical thinking capacities and expands rather than limits their potentials. This implies moving decisively beyond the discourse of basic skills mastery and proficiency testing. As for vocational or occupational education, an effort must be made to ensure that it moves beyond narrow job preparation or socialization. Joe Kincheloe (1995) suggests that vocationalism be replaced with a critical "work education," the purpose of which would be "to restore the knowledge of the work process and the overview of the relation of the job to the larger economic processes" (p. 61). According to Kincheloe, "The critical dimension of work education involves the skill to interrogate the democratic limits of both work and the capitalist economy" (p. 322). In a similar vein, Simon, Dippo, and Schenke (1991) advocate what they call "critical work pedagogy," the aim of which is "to encourage students to: question taken-for-granted assumptions about work; comprehend workplaces as sites where identities are produced; see this production as a struggle over competing claims to truth and to correctness; and envisage ways in whch the quality of their working lives can be improved" (p. 15). The college preparatory track is, in many ways, moving in the right direction already with a shift to a constructivist curriculum. Here the challenge is to develop ways of reducing the individualistic, grade-oriented competition that is so pervasive among college preparatory students by developing more cooperative and group learning projects, including community service learning projects.

What about magnet schools? Is there a place in a democratic progressive agenda to support magnet schools? Here I think the answer must be, "It depends." It depends very much on how magnet schools are institutionalized within local districts. Timothy Young and Evans Clinchy (1992), in their examination of choice plans in education, suggest that "the best approach is to make all district schools alternative or magnets and allow students to choose the school or program they prefer" (p. 26). In such a system, access to a school would not be restricted by admission requirements, inadequate dissemination of information to parents and students, or lack of transportation. Continual efforts also would be needed to counter tendencies of magnet schools to become segregated by class, race, or gender. Finally, in order to promote dialogue and community by students across their differences, several magnet schools might be located on a common campus, with some courses and projects designed to bring students from different magnets together to explore common concerns and develop a more inclusive sense of community.

Another idea that is worth pursuing, and that embodies some of the advantages of a magnet school system but overcomes some of its limitations, is to divide comprehensive neighborhood high schools into "school-within-a-school" units. Each of these schools-within-a-school may have its own identity and curricular focus, and even an admission process, but also maintain a heterogeneous grouping of students. A good example of this is the "charter" school reform movement in Philadelphia in the 1990s, in which old comprehensive high schools are being broken up into smaller, heterogeneously grouped schools, organized around shared decision making (Fine, 1994). In charter schools, anywhere from 200 to 400 students work with a group of 10 to 12 core subject teachers over the course of the 4 years of high school. Charter school teachers enjoy a common preparation period daily, and it is the responsibility of teachers in each charter to invent curriculum, pedagogies, and "substantive themes" that give that charter its unique character. Charter schools are, in fact, an attempt to create semiautonomous communities of learners in public high schools and overcome one of the major impediments to providing personalized instruction in the "old" comprehensive high school—the great and ever-changing number of students teachers interacted with daily. Among the payoffs of the switch to charter schools has been better attendance records and lower dropout rates. Similar school-within-a-school programs are cropping up in school districts across the country and are proving to be particularly effective in improving achievement levels and lowering dropout rates among low-achieving, inner-city youth.

Unfortunately, all of these reforms are only palliatives as long as the underlying forces that perpetuate tracking practices remain unaddressed. It is naive to believe that public schools can be detracked outside of a broad-based movement for democratic renewal in the culture, including a movement toward a more equitable economy and an improvement in the quality of people's working lives. Certainly, there is much room within public schools in which to work for democratic change. However, we cannot expect public schools to be detracked so long as schools continue to be implicated in preparing young people for such inequitable futures. This means devoting more of our attention to improving the quality and the pay of many existing jobs and doing still more to overcome inequalities of opportunity in the work force. It also may imply a commitment to full employment and to macroeconomic policies designed to create a broad range of jobs and to counter current trends toward a two-tiered economy. Over the past decade, neoconservative and neoliberal reformers have blamed schools for many of the troubles of the economy. If only schools could turn out more high-skilled workers, then, according to this logic, there would be fewer low-skill, low-paying jobs in the economy. Supposedly, business was ready and willing to hire high-quality, high-skilled, high-wage workers, if only the schools would turn them out. The truth is that major corporations and businesses have not invested in job development as they should, but have preferred short-term profits through the hiring of more low-skilled, temporary, and part-time employees (Johnson, 1993). A democratic progressive discourse that is serious about detracking will need to be integrated with a new economic policy discourse that begins to talk seriously about countering the growing inequalities that divide us as a society and as a people.

4

Constructing the Margins

Of Multicultural Education
and Curriculum Settlements

IN PROFESSIONAL EDUCATIONAL discourse the public school curriculum often is viewed as a corpus of "basic skills" or "essential knowledge" that everyone needs to know. Broad consensus is presumed to exist about the goals of education and even the specific "learning objectives" that should be targeted in each subject area. Within this taken-for-granted discursive framework, much energy is devoted to discussion of how to more effectively and efficiently deliver the prescribed curriculum and evaluate the extent to which students have "mastered" it. This treatment of knowledge in a reified and structural manner has the effect of depoliticizing decisions about what is taught in the schools since it explicitly directs our attention away from the recognition that knowledge is socially constructed. Knowledge does not exist in some abstract, "objective" form but rather emerges out of cultural struggle, serves some groups more than others, and is deployed within a dynamic field of action to either affirm or challenge dominant power relations. The public school curriculum, from this constructivist perspective, may be appreciated as a negotiated compromise or settlement between dominant and marginalized power blocs and social movements concerning what "truths" will be taught in the schools, whose knowledge will be privileged, what voices will be heard and silenced, and how knowledge or "truth" is to be arrived at.

In what follows, I want to explore some of the implications of viewing the public school curriculum as a knowledge settlement by focusing on an analysis of multicultural education. The historical emergence of multicultural education as a curriculum subfield over the past several decades has been related to a settlement between civil rights groups and the state, with the state agreeing, in effect, to make positive efforts to make the public school curriculum more inclu-

A somewhat modified version of this chapter was published as "Constructing the Margins: Of Multicultural Education and Curriculum Settlements" by D. Carlson, 1995, *Curriculum Inquiry, 25*, pp. 407–432.

sive of the cultural diversity of U.S. society, validate the culture and language of minority and socioeconomically disadvantaged students, and promote greater sensitivity to the perspectives of various Others in society and thus fight bigotry and discriminatory treatment. In recent years, multicultural education has been expanded somewhat in response to pressure from the women's movement to include in the curriculum issues of gender equity and the recognition of women's contributions to culture and history. Nevertheless, the basic discursive framework that guides the field, particularly in K–12 public education, has not changed much since the late 1960s. In a number of ways that I want to explore in this chapter, multicultural education has not been very successful in overcoming the marginalization and alienation of minority students or building a diverse democratic community in the schools. Of course, things might be much worse without multicultural education. Making the "Other" visible in the curriculum has been a major accomplishment; and multicultural education has provided an important "space" within the school program to explicitly address issues of race, class, and gender identity. At the same time, multicultural education in its current form has been incorporated within dominant professional discourses in education in ways that block its fuller potential in building a democratic, multicultural society and in helping marginalized students construct empowering identities. Specifically, I want to argue, multicultural education has been limited by a number of discursive blockages. It has been structurally marginalized within the overall curriculum program; it has treated identity in a reified manner rather than as socially and historically constructed; it has treated prejudicial beliefs as merely individual psychological phenomena rather than as implicated in power relations that privilege some and disempower others; and it has integrated multicultural education within dominant pedagogical practices in the school rather than linking it with a critical pedagogy based on dialogue and constructivist conceptions of knowledge and identity. In these ways, multicultural education has participated in educational practices that continue to define and locate various "others" at the margins of power.

In the 1990s, as the economic, cultural, and educational terrain is being reshaped, and as we move into an unstable and unsettling age, multicultural education is under increasing attack from a number of political directions. The various new social movements of identity on the democratic left have begun to call into question the gains made through existing multicultural education programs. They also have begun to articulate a new language of empowerment and have challenged the notion that there is one way of knowing the truth and even one truth to be known. The assertion of feminist and Afrocentric ways of knowing, for example, has profound implications in challenging "objectivist" notions of knowledge that prevail in public schools. Meanwhile, those on the political right have begun to call more unabashedly for a return to a Eurocentric and male-centric curriculum in public schools and challenge the supposed "political correctness'' fostered by "radical" multiculturalism on campuses (D'Souza, 1991). Multicultural education, then, has become a major terrain of struggle in the 1990s, and democratic and progressive forces will need to both defend multicultural education and call for its radical reconstruction. In this regard, I want to speculate on some of the principles that might guide a democratic progressive resettlement of multicultural education for new times.

OF THE STATE, POLICY SETTLEMENTS, AND UNSETTLING TIMES

The notion that state policy and reform initiatives represent and express "settlements" between dominant and oppositional groups takes on meaning only within a broader discourse; so I want to begin by mapping out some of the assumptions and principles that, in a general way, characterize this theoretical discourse, which I will refer to as neo-Gramscian. By neo-Gramscian I mean that it is grounded in the work of the early-twentieth-century Italian social theorist Antonio Gramsci but appropriates Gramscian insights within a poststructural analysis of the state and of economic, cultural, and political developments in the late twentieth century (Gramsci, 1971; Hall & Jacques, 1990; Morrow, 1991). The state, as Gramsci saw it, was a series of loosely connected governmental sites at various tiers where the leadership of dominant groups was played out and struggled over. The structuralist notion of a unified "ruling class" that controls the state is replaced with the more historically accurate notion of a power bloc— a ruling alliance of social movements, composed of different factions that are loosely held together to assume leadership in the state and civil society—what Gramsci called hegemony. However loosely a ruling power bloc is held together, in the process of constructing hegemony it must articulate a commonsense view of the public interest that becomes widely accepted in all levels of civil society. This commonsense discourse on social values, goals, and problems then provides a set of slogans, principles, and themes that legitimate state policy as serving the broad public interest rather than the special interests of dominant groups in the power bloc. Thus, the power of the state may be dispersed across various semiautonomous tiers (local, state, federal) and further dispersed among legislative, executive, judicial, military, police, health, welfare, and education agencies; yet state policy across tiers and sites has cohesiveness because of the influence of a commonsense discourse on reform that becomes widely taken for granted at all levels (Dale, 1989).

Gramsci also recognized that no hegemony is ever complete. Rather, it is always partial and incomplete, always in the process of being advanced in the face of resistance and opposition by counterhegemonic alliances engaged in an ongoing "war of maneuver" for leadership of the state (Gramsci, 1971). This also implies that hegemony is negotiated; and this is where the notion of settlements enters the picture. According to Gramsci, to help prevent counterhegemonic blocs from mobilizing, hegemonic power blocs had to take account of "those interests and tendencies of the groups over which hegemony is to be exercised," so that "a certain compromise should be formed" (quoted in Hall, 1988, p. 133). Stuart Hall and other so-called New Times scholars working in this tradition in the United Kingdom have referred to these compromises as "accords" or "settlements." Through settlements, minority and marginalized groups are able to make incursions into the mainstream of the political process and open up space in the state for progressive change, even though they are not part of the power bloc that exercises leadership in the state (Apple, 1988; Omi & Winant, 1986). At the same time, settlements serve to incorporate discontent within parameters that do not seriously threaten the privilege of dominant groups. This means that settlements embody contradictions that generate contradictory outcomes. These contradictions, along with changes in the terrain of cultural and political struggle, ultimately lead to an "unsettling" of settlements and their renegotiation in ways that either advance or roll back gains made by marginalized groups.

According to Hall and others, stability in the post–World War II era in Great Britain (and to some extent throughout advanced capitalist societies) was constructed around a number of core, interlocking social policy settlements. These included, perhaps most centrally, an *industrial* settlement. Semiskilled factory workers accepted workplace subordination and job rationalization in return for state-regulated, collective-bargaining rights that provided job security and a relatively high standard of living, which made possible a new consumer society, which led to more productivity and higher profits. This settlement was intertwined with a *social settlement* that vastly expanded public services and the welfare safety net for those victimized by structural unemployment and shifts in the labor market. The postwar *gender settlement* was one that expelled women from the labor force and returned them to the home. Since working-class men were guaranteed a family wage through the industrial settlement, women became the focus of consumption. Finally, a *racial settlement* allowed former colonial peoples to immigrate to Great Britain for the first time, although once there they were economically exploited in the growing service industry. Obviously, none of these settlements resolved deep-rooted conflicts among dominant and marginalized groups. However, they did provide the foundation for an "unstable equilibrium" in political leadership throughout the 1950s and 1960s.

Because they are tentative, contested, and undermined by contradictions, and because culture is dynamic rather than static, settlements are prone to periodically come unsettled. At particular historic junctures, new hegemonic discourses on reform may emerge that are based on significant rewritings of settlements and consistent with the emergence of a new power bloc. Gramsci recognized that the "fordist" society he saw emerging in the early twentieth century—with the shift toward large-scale industrial development, centralized bureaucratic management, and a new popular culture organized around consumption and mass markets—was leading to an unsettling time in European politics. That unsettling time provided the basis for building new hegemonic movements on the left (democratic and bureaucratic state socialism) as well as the "authoritarian populist" right (fascism) (Gramsci, 1971; Rustin, 1989). That is, the transition to a "fordist" society did not lead to a predetermined political outcome; but it did set the stage upon which new power blocs were mobilized and new settlements constructed.

In a similar way, neo-Gramscian scholars have used the term "post-fordism" to refer to changes going on in the economic and cultural spheres at the current time that are leading to an unsettling of post–World War II social policy settlements. The most defining characteristic of the new post-fordist world is economic restructuring. As production has become dispersed globally (particularly to the "Third World"), the United States and other advanced capitalist societies have become increasingly two-tiered and inequitable, with minorities and women clustered in the lower tier of semiskilled workers (Mayer, 1991). Post-fordism also implies a reconfiguration and fragmentation of political power blocs. New technologies, along with the pervasiveness of television, have made it possible for social movements to organize both nationally and locally to exert pressure on public institutions outside the framework of the two-party political system (Escobar, 1992; Melucci, 1989a). On the political left, "identity politics" (the archetypal politics of the postmodern era) involves struggles by groups marginalized or disempowered by class, gender, race, sexuality, handicappism, and so forth, to challenge negative representations of their identities in popular culture, fight discrimination, and construct and affirm empowering forms of collective identification (Bromley, 1989). These new social movements both are responses to, and call into being, new social movements on the political right, including fundamentalist Christian coalitions, the "Right to Life" movement, "family values" groups, and so forth, organized around the defense of traditionalist, authoritarian, and patriarchal forms of identity and in opposition to "special rights" for marginalized groups. Multicultural education, I want to suggest, has emerged out of and taken on meaning within this shifting terrain of cultural struggle in the late twentieth century.

MULTICULTURAL EDUCATION AS A CURRICULUM SETTLEMENT

This perspective on the state as a site of struggle, social policy settlements, and the changing economic, political, and cultural terrain of the late twentieth century, has important implications for how we analyze state educational policy and curriculum reform movements. At the most general level, it calls for an analysis of how the curriculum has emerged out of struggle organized around class, gender, race, and other power dynamics, and how hegemonic discourses in education have sought to address the concerns and incorporate the interests of marginalized groups through the adoption of formal policy and the institutionalization of special programs and curriculum revisions. For example, during the fordist era in the early decades of the century, the public school curriculum in the United States was constructed consistent with a number of class, gender, and racial settlements. Vocational education, supported in the Smith–Hughes Act of 1917, was the outcome of a settlement between the business community and organized labor, with both groups participating in overseeing the development of vocational education programs designed to provide working-class boys with job training for the skilled trades and working-class girls with clerical training. Outside of vocational education, the "general" track in the comprehensive high school also represented a settlement of sorts. Little was expected of students in the way of rigorous engagement with subject matter, and the curriculum focused on social and work discipline skills. Students merely had to stay in school and graduate in order to get a job with a "living wage" in industry. As more and more women were drawn out of the labor force in the 1950s and as the "family wage" allowed working-class men to support a nuclear family, the dominant gender settlement for both working- and middle-class girls emphasized instruction in home economics, "life adjustment," and "family life" education. The dominant racial settlement in public education throughout the first half of the century was one that provided a watered down curriculum and technical education to African Americans through a system of segregated schools—a settlement that began to be challenged in profound ways in the 1950s.

These curriculum settlements began to change somewhat as the shift toward de-industrialization, post-fordist economic organization, and a two-tiered socioeconomic order began to accelerate in the late 1960s. Within this context, the state began to be pressured by business leadership to do a better job of teaching the "functional literacy" and computational skills needed in the new service industry and in clerical jobs in which workers had to interface with computer technologies (Carlson, 1993). At the same time, the schools were under pressure from civil rights groups to assume a much greater role in countering the socioeconomic inequalities being fostered by the new economic order and providing an academic climate in which inner-city youth, many of them racial minorities, could succeed. The major curriculum reform settlement that emerged out of the confluence of these developments and pressures was compensatory or remedial education, as formalized at the federal level in "Title I" of the Elementary and Secondary Education Act (ESEA) of 1965. Title I provided funds to local districts to establish special programs to help raise achievement levels in schools with a high proportion of socioeconomically disadvantaged youth, with a strong emphasis on output-based, "basic skills" approaches to remediation. It was designed to promote higher achievement among disadvantaged youth by facilitating smaller classes and more individual attention, it committed the schools to the notion that all students can achieve at least minimum standards, and it held teachers and school districts accountable for raising achievement levels. However, compensatory and remedial programs have been limited in their capacity to empower marginalized students, for several reasons. They have been incorporated within a hegemonic discourse that locates the source of academic underachievement within the "skill deficits" and cultural background of the child and thus participates in "blaming the victim" (Ryan, 1971). They also have been institutionalized within a system of tracking and ability grouping, and they have had the effect of isolating "at-risk" students in low-ability groups and noncredit classes (Oakes, 1985; Page, 1991). Once tracked in remedial classes, disadvantaged youth rarely get ahead; and those who do acquire the "basics" face economic disempowerment in the bottom tier of an increasingly inequitable labor force.

Partially as a way of countering some of these limitations in compensatory education programs, and in order to respond to growing pressure from African American, Hispanic, and women's groups to make the curriculum more inclusive and representative, a new curriculum settlement began to emerge in U.S. public schools around the notion of multicultural education. A few school districts scattered across the nation were beginning to institutionalize "bicultural," "multiethnic," "multiracial," and "bilingual" programs by the late 1960s, but it was not until the mid- to late 1970s that many states began requiring or recommending that local school districts develop instructional objectives related to "teaching cultural diversity," "understanding the contributions of diverse peoples to American society," "promoting sensitivity to cultural differences," and so on (Cummins, 1992; Gay, 1983). The birth of multicultural education as a professional educational field of research and curriculum development may be pegged to the acknowledgment of "multicultural education" as a descriptor in the 1977–1978 volume of *Education Index*, which included 62 references to articles in the field. The term *multicultural education* has been used in professional discourse to designate a broad range of related programs, classes, and curricular materials, including "pull-out" bilingual and bicultural education classes for Hispanic students; African American and women's history months and elective classes; revisions in history textbooks and literary anthologies to include the contributions of minorities and women; and values clarification and moral education classes and workshops designed to teach reciprocity, respect for difference, and conflict resolution (Sleeter & Grant, 1987).

In all of these various forms, multicultural education generally has been grounded in a discourse that is based on two basic premises. The first of these premises is that by affirming marginalized students' cultural and linguistic backgrounds in the school curriculum, we can enhance their self-concepts and hence their academic success. The second is that dominant-culture students can be taught to be less prejudicial and more sensitive to the rights and perspectives of marginalized students, which will have the effect of making marginalized students feel less alienated, which will enhance their academic success. Both of these premises, it seems to me, represent a significant advancement over the deficit theory that underlies compensatory and remedial approaches to meeting the needs of marginalized youth; and this suggests that multicultural education may provide a much more viable space within the school curriculum for advancing democratic and progressive projects aimed at the construction of empowering identities among marginalized youth. Like compensatory and remedial education, however, multicultural education has been partially incorporated within neoconservative and neoliberal discourses in ways that currently block its fuller democratic potential. As a result, there is little evidence that dominant-culture students' attitudes toward various marginalized Others changes significantly after exposure to a multicultural education program. According to Cameron McCarthy (1990), "Various pretest–post-test evaluations of multicultural education and human relations programs that emphasize attitudinal change and cultural understanding suggest that these programs have not been very successful in achieving their espoused goal of eliminating majority/minority prejudice" (p. 45). I now want to examine these limitations or blockages in more detail, with the intent of speculating on how they might be countered in articulating a democratic progressive reform discourse.

The Marginalization of Multicultural Education in the Curriculum

In an ironic and contradictory way, multicultural education typically has been institutionalized within the curriculum and within public schools in ways that affirm the boundaries between the center and the margins of the curriculum. One way in which multicultural education is marginalized is by incorporating it within a highly "classified" curriculum, in which there are many separate, discrete subject areas and units of study, and a highly "framed" curriculum, in which each subject area is rigidly insulated from others (Bernstein, 1975). Within such a highly classified and framed curriculum, multicultural education has been assigned a marginalized and isolated space, insulated from the core subject areas of math, science, English, and social studies. As such, it represents a means of absorbing and insulating demands for change in the curriculum by confining change to one ancillary subject area. For example, multicultural education may be limited to the recognition of African American History Month, or to special units in social studies classes on the contributions of minorities and women, or to a special human relations workshop on respecting differences, conducted once each year by a counselor. This structural marginalization is representative of the value placed on multicultural education and of the belief that it is just one more "subject" or set of learning objectives among many, for which some limited time and space must be found in a very crowded curriculum. One way we can begin moving beyond the structural marginalization of multicultural education is to move toward a curriculum that is not rigidly classified and framed. Multidisciplinary approaches would facilitate the integration of multicultural education throughout the curriculum.

Marginalization also may be expressed through tokenistic forms of inclusion. This largely has been the case in the much-touted revision of the literary "canon" to include works by women and people of color. The revision of the canon, and the concurrent changes in literary anthologies used in schools, has come about largely because public schools and state boards of education have adopted antiracist and antisexist guidelines for textbook adoption. This change represents substantial progress in a relatively short time frame. However, if inclusion in the canon is preferable to exclusion, it nevertheless leaves something to be desired since it often takes the form of tokenism. Major high school literature anthologies continue to include primarily the works of dead, white, Anglo-Saxon males, with a few minority and women authors added (Sleeter & Grant, 1991). Furthermore, as Russell Ferguson (1990) observes, "the demand for admission to the canon remains a contradictory project, because it implies an acceptance of essential features of the existing structure" (p. 10). The "canonizing" of literature is inextricably involved in defining the cultural center and the margin, since it holds up certain works as important and representative of the culture as a whole and relegates others to the margins. All categories based on inclusion also require categories based on exclusion—a relegation to the less important or worthy of attention. Rather than seek inclusion into a canon that defines and fixes the cultural center, it may be more democratic to call into question the very idea of a canon, or at least of a single literary canon. This means breaking down the artificial boundaries that divide "popular culture" from "high culture" and that privilege the latter in the curriculum. In pushing for a resettlement of multicultural education, we might emphasize less reliance on anthologies that include "token" minority and women authors, and more choice within a broad range of literary texts, including significant contributions by women, African Americans, Hispanics, and others.

Yet another way in which multicultural education may be marginalized is through spatial isolation. This often occurs geographically, with urban schools serving large proportions of minority students most likely to have classes, workshops, and activities organized around the theme of multicultural education. In mostly white, middle-class suburbs, multicultural education often can hardly be said to be practiced at all, aside from formal recognition of African American History Month or Martin Luther King Day. This reinforces a belief that multicultural education is for minority students and that other students do not need it since "their" (white, middle-class) culture is already represented in the curriculum. In fact, one could argue that it is white, middle-class students who need multicultural education the most—that is, need to begin thinking beyond the notion of a dominant Eurocentric culture that ''allows'' various other subcultures to exist at the margins.

The spatial marginalization of multicultural education also may be expressed within the space of classrooms; the speaker panel provides perhaps the best example of this. At the college level, speaker panels of African American, Hispanic, women, or gay and lesbian students often are invited to classes to talk about the African American, Hispanic, women's, or gay ''experience'' and to field questions from students. As a one-time activity designed to fulfill multicultural education requirements, the speaker panel enacts an elaborate ritual of spatial marginalization and distancing. The three or four individuals who typically constitute a speaker panel are almost always positioned at the front of the class, often on a special stage in large college classes. Under the anonymous gaze of students who are transformed into interrogators in this ritual, marginalized students are made visible at last—but only on a stage that serves as a spatial representation of distancing. Thus speaker panels still position students in ways that promote ''them'' versus ''us'' thinking and that separate and isolate the Other at a safe distance. We will need to reconceptualize space within the classroom in order to move beyond the spatial marginalization of the Other that is represented in speaker panels. The speaker panel makes use of a traditional arrangement of learning space, with someone ''on stage'' at the front of the class and all chairs organized in rows facing the classroom stage. Democratic forms of multicultural education need to be grounded in dialogue in which all participate; and this necessitates a more circular, informal construction of space.

The Essentialistic Treatment of Identity

To treat a category essentialistically means to view it as ''natural'' and ''given'' rather than as socially constructed within the context of power dynamics. Essentializing erects rigid boundaries and borders around categories of collective identity (race, class, gender, sexual orientation, etc.) and encourages us to presume that these categories are unified, static, and objective descriptors of natural difference. We are also more likely to unwittingly position categories of class, race, gender, and sexual identity within bipolar oppositional constructs that set high expectations for one pole (middle class, white, male, heterosexual) and low or marginalized expectations for the other pole. Racial categories in the United States provide a good example of a socially constructed bipolar opposition (white/Black) that typically has been treated essentialistically. In fact, race as an important identity category did not really appear on the historical scene before the age of European colonialization and American slavery, when races were constructed as part of the project of European colonialism, with the "white" race placed at the center of culture, civilization, and modernization, and various other races constructed at the margins (either nearer or farther from the center). In the United States, as Cornel West (1990) has observed, European immigrants arrived as "Irish," "Sicilian," or "Lithuanian," and had to have their identities reconstituted in the assimilation process—a process in which African Americans played an important role: "They [European immigrants] had to learn that they were 'White' principally by adopting an American discourse of positively-valued Whiteness and negatively-charged Blackness" (p. 29). In U.S. history, then, the identities of marginalized racial and linguistic groups have been constructed in the dominant culture as everything that whites are not (criminal, dirty, promiscuous, etc.), and this construction of identity has been used to legitimate discriminatory and oppressive practices.

Essentialistic treatment of identity has been common in developmental psychology, since developmentalism provides a rationale for arguing that some groups are at a lower developmental level than others and should not be pushed to excel academically since they lack the capacity for abstract reasoning. For example, Granville Stanley Hall, an early-twentieth-century developmental psychologist who had a significant impact on curriculum reform, was a strong believer that education for African Americans and Native Americans must respect their "natural" differences from whites. Hall argued that education for African Americans should respect their "unique gifts of intense emotional endowment, capacity for merriment, patience, submissiveness, mysticism, and primitive sense of rhythm" (Curti, 1959, p. 413). Some multicultural education discourses also have come alarmingly close to essentializing identity in similar ways, I think, when arguing that racial and linguistic minority students have a preferred "learning style" different from that of middle-class, white students. For example, in the 1970s and 1980s, a number of studies applied psychological theories of *field-independent* and *field-dependent* learning to characterize the differing learning styles of racial and ethnic groups in the United States (Nieto, 1992; Witkin, 1962). Field-independent individuals supposedly learn best in situations that emphasize analytic thinking skills and in abstract and hypothetical situations. Field-dependent learners, in contrast, learn best in cooperative social settings, focusing on specific examples, concrete applications, and hands-on experience. Research based on this bipolar learning theory generally led to the conclusion that white students are the most field-independent learners, while Mexican American, Native American, and African American students tend to be closer to the field-dependent learning style (Ramirez & Castaneda, 1974).

It is certainly true that culture influences the way we reason about the world and construct meaning, so we would expect that individuals with differing cultural backgrounds would probably think through problems in somewhat differing ways. It also seems to follow that these differing learning styles should be taken into account in education, since education needs to be compatible with students' existing ways of knowing and expressing knowing. However, young people also need to be challenged to think in new and different ways if they are to be empowered. We must remember that ways of knowing are not merely culture-specific traits; they are culturally produced within the context of power inequalities. The field-dependent learning style, for example, historically is associated with the work experience of those at the bottom of the labor hierarchy. This means that we may participate in the reproduction of inequality if we emphasize concrete, manually oriented, noncompetitive learning styles for minority students that socialize them for one kind of labor, while we emphasize an entirely different, competitive, abstract learning style for those we expect to go on to college and enter the professional-managerial class. Given existing economic realities, theories of alternative learning styles seem likely to be incorporated within discourses and practices in schools that distinguish between high- and low-ability students and between college-bound and general or vocational track students.

Some critical or radical discourses in multicultural education, associated with identity politics, also have essentialized identity—particularly race and gender identity. Since the mid-1980s a movement has been growing among African American educators and community leaders for some form of "Afrocentric" curriculum for African American students that not only reclaims the roots of African American culture in African history and culture but also takes into account the culture-specific world view and epistemology of the African people. Afrocentric "magnet" schools within the public school system as well as private Afrocentric schools are beginning to be organized in many major U.S. cities. The notion of Afrocentricity has been used in the literature to refer to a number of similar tenets. One author summarizes these tenets as follows: "Human beings are conceived collectively; human beings are spiritual; human beings are good; the affective approach to knowledge is epistemologically valid; much of human behavior is nonrational; [and] the axiology or highest value lies in interpersonal relations" (Schiele, 1990, p. 147). Another author suggests that an Afrocentric world view "would be based upon three traditional values: harmony with nature, humaneness, and rhythm" (Covin, 1990, p. 127). Similarly, feminist perspectives have emphasized the importance of an epistemology based on caring, connectedness, intuitive or holistic thinking, cooperation, dialogue, voice, and so on, and the 1990s have seen calls for the establishment of schools based on feminist epistemologies (Noddings, 1992).

The discourses of Afrocentrism and feminism have been important in their recognition that epistemologies are culturally and historically specific, that oppositional epistemologies always exist, and that we can and must move beyond patriarchal, Eurocentric, and capitalist mindsets in order to empower marginalized students. The problem is that these alternative world views, epistemologies, and paradigms tend to get reduced to a simplistic dichotimization of ways of knowing and being-in-the-world that begins to look very predictable. Within this bipolar opposition, marginalized epistemologies (whether African American or feminist) are seen to represent one set of "positive" values—cooperation, caring, connectedness to the earth, analysis of concrete situations, relational thinking, equity, and so on—while the dominant epistemology is portrayed as representing another set of "negative" values—individualism, competition, hierarchy, bureaucratic or technical rationality, objectivist thinking, inequality, and so on. In effect, then, marginalized epistemologies tend to be constructed at least partially out of the experience of subordination, rather than out of some authentic racial or gendered self. Many of the values held by subordinated groups are important in advancing democratic projects, but in order to move away from bipolar oppositional power relations and forms of identity construction, we will need to view these values as less oppositional and not neatly arrayed in two sets. This means that we must be very careful not to essentialize Afrocentric and feminist epistemologies, but rather view them as historically emergent within the context of power relations of domination and subordination. Along with this, we must be on guard against dividing students into two camps: whites and Blacks, or males and females, or heterosexuals and homosexuals, which are defined through bipolar oppositions. One way postmodern theorists suggest we may begin seeing individuals more complexly is to recognize that we all occupy *multiple subject positions*. That is, we have a gender, a race, ethnicity, class, sexual orientation, and so forth. Because we *are* all of these "selves," we are embroiled in a number of different power relations and cultural struggles simultaneously, all of which influence the way we know the world and all of which interrelate in a complex, nonsynchronous, and sometimes contradictory manner in identity formation (McCarthy, 1988).

The Treatment of Discrimination and Bias as Individual Cognitive-Psychological Phenomena

Since individuals decide who they are only within the context of culture and take on their identities only in relation to Others, individuals are not autonomous actors—as the liberal Enlightenment tradition presumed. Not only is subjectivity constructed relationally, it is constructed within cultural discourses on identity. For example, dominant discourses in U.S. society contain taken-for-granted beliefs about white, male, middle-class, heterosexual superiority that are used to legitimate privilege. Subjectivities (and hence identities) constructed within these discourses contain a "deep structure" of bias and privilege. This does not mean that individuals in dominant groups inevitably or deterministically must represent bias and privilege in their everyday use of language and interaction with Others. For one thing, all cultural discourses contain contradictions and oppositional beliefs and values. Thus, Eurocentric discourses contain within them reservoirs of democratic beliefs organized around social justice, equity, community, freedom, and so on; and white people may use these beliefs and values to work through racist beliefs and side with the oppressed. The experience of members of dominant groups with racial Others, or their personal experience with discrimination as poor, female, gay, and so forth, also may lead them to discard stereotypes and bias. Still, all of this occurs within the context of culture and power relations with Others. A poststructural account of the personal would consider the individual not as an isolated, autonomous monad but as both the producer and product of culture (Sullivan, 1984). This means that efforts to treat bias and discrimination as merely individual problems, the result of individual deficiencies in cognitive development or "moral reasoning," have the effect of diverting our attention away from the need to challenge dominant discourses of privilege.

Within multicultural education the individualization of bias and discrimination has been a pervasive theme, particularly in the professional discourse on "moral education" that has borrowed heavily from the cognitive developmental theories of Jean Piaget (1970) and Lawrence Kohlberg (1981). Very briefly, Piaget's developmental theory of intelligence is based on the proposition that cognitive growth is associated with a gradual shift from *egocentric* thinking, in which the individual sees the world only from his or her perspective, to *formal operational*, abstract, or universalistic thinking. Beginning in the concrete operational years of preadolescence, and developing most fully in the formal operational years of adolescence and adulthood, the individual is presumed to be able to develop empathy for the Other by rising above his or her subject position and viewing the situation from either the perspective of a disinterested party or the perspective of the Other. According to David Elkind (1974), a leading interpreter of Piaget's work for educators, "from the developmental point of view . . . egocentrism can be regarded as a *negative* by-product of any emergent mental system" (p. 74; emphasis added). Through the process of abstraction and distancing from the self, students gradually learn the importance of the "golden rule" of reciprocity or equal treatment of individuals. This basic Piagetian model of decentering provided Kohlberg with the framework within which to construct a more specific but essentially similar theory of moral development and reasoning. Kohlberg proposed that the development of moral reasoning begins at the "preconventional" level where issues are resolved from a purely egocentric, reward and punishment orientation; advances to the "conventional" level where judgments are made according to conventional or prescribed norms; and culminates at the "postconventional" level where judgments reflect legalistic conceptions of individual rights and universalistic moral principles.

Multicultural education, in these terms, is about becoming a member of a democratic, diverse society through affirmation of a social contract with fellow citizens and adherence to rules of reciprocity. It is also, in the words of one

Piagetian educator, about "constructing an objective view of society . . . [that] coordinates all the perspectives of the different members of society into one generalized perspective—an achievement of adolescence or adulthood" (Edwards, 1986, p. 141). What are some of the programmatic implications of this cognitive psychology discourse for multicultural education? According to one article in a professional journal for social studies teachers, when confronted with a question about social justice and discriminatory treatment, children may be encouraged to "practice the skill of 'reversibility'; a reversible moral decision is one that is right from anyone's perspective" (Gallaher, 1988, p. 528). In a recent article on moral development and sex equity, Sandra Styer (1988) describes a number of moral dilemmas that have been used to challenge sexism in the elementary grades. One of these explores the fairness of a "middle-grade teacher who sent only girls as helpers to the kindergarten although one boy wished to go." In another hypothetical situation, children were asked "whether it was wrong to have a male doctor talk only to the boys and a female nurse talk only to the girls" (p. 175).

These approaches to multicultural education certainly have their merits. They help students learn that prejudicial and stereotypical thinking misrepresents reality, they inject issues of ethics and justice into human practice, and they affirm the central role of the educative process in countering oppressive belief systems. Nevertheless, there are some serious problems with Piagetian and Kohlbergian approaches that need to be addressed. Let me begin with the notion that cognitive development moves individuals toward a more "enlightened" or rational assessment of society and a more tolerant and humanistic regard for the Other. While reason is a powerful tool that can help lead us toward a more just and equitable society, we must be careful not to accept unproblematically this Cartesian or Enlightenment ideal, for it may lead us to overemphasize the effect of more education per se, or the development of "higher-order" thinking skills, in overcoming social bias and promoting social justice. If education alone was what made people more just, humane, and democratic, middle-class Republicans would be the most "enlightened" members of society, since they are among the most educated.

As I indicated at the outset, the individualization of bias and discrimination, by locating bigotry and "narrow-mindedness" in the irrational beliefs of individuals operating at lower levels of cognitive development, diverts our attention away from seeing that individual subjectivities are constructed within dominant discourses of power and knowledge and that prejudicial beliefs support privilege. Thus, it is not just an end to "irrational," prejudicial thinking that is called for, it is the end of privilege—and it is this privilege that needs to be confronted as much as or more than beliefs. Yet, the discourse of moral education is explicitly designed not to raise issues of privilege that might threaten members of dominant groups. Thus, Styer (1988) argues that hypothetical moral dilemmas counter gender bias and discrimination without making boys feel uncomfortable and that the "possibility that sex equity dilemmas might . . . threaten males more in the classroom can be alleviated by careful and systematic construction and discussion of dilemmas that portray a balanced proportion of males and females behaving in sex-biased ways" (p. 173). It may be comforting to males, but hardly very insightful or politically empowering (for women at least), to present gender relations in American culture in terms of men and women who are equally bigoted. The fact that this type of curriculum is nonthreatening is thus constructed as one of its "selling points," and this suggests that it has tended to become incorporated within the school's conflict resolution and management goals. The avoidance of overt conflict in the classroom also may be related to the use of hypothetical rather than real, concrete moral dilemmas that confront young people in their everyday lives. A democratic resettlement of multicultural education, rather than attempting to mute conflict and tension in the classroom, would look to the classroom as a safe space for students to confront one another across their differences and work through their conflicts in a direct, personal dialogue that intermixes reasoning, feeling, and valuing. We cannot rise above our subject positions to some neutral, objective, rational spot where we can decide how to "do the right thing" by invoking universalistic, abstract, moral principles; but we can provide a space in schools for dialogue across difference, and we can work on building alliances to fight specific cases of inequity and privilege.

The Failure to Ground Multicultural Education in a Critical Pedagogy

Throughout the past several decades, all state-sponsored educational reforms have been made to fit within a discourse on instructional effectiveness and mastery of predetermined learning outcomes. Within this reform context, multicultural education has been translated into "learning outputs" and "pupil performance objectives," with curriculum materials and textbooks designed to help teachers teach to these objectives. A more democratic and progressive multicultural education would need to be built on a critical pedagogy that helps students reflect upon their own identity formation, actively participate in constructing empowering identities, and engage in dialogue and action with Others. Thus it would need to acknowledge the central role of the teacher, the pedagogic encounter, and the construction of knowledge and meaning within the context of that encounter. By speaking about multicultural education as if it were merely a curriculum to be delivered to students by anonymous teachers in standardized ways, we focus attention away from pedagogy and the active construction of meaning in the classroom, and this may have the effect of limiting the potential of multicultural education to empower students.

In moving beyond this limitation, democratic and progressive forces in education may well look to what is going on in higher education. Within the context of pressure from minority and women's student groups and faculty, and insulated by the tradition of academic freedom and critical scholarship at the university, multicultural education has begun to move in quite different directions than it has in the public schools. In very basic terms, this has involved the articulation of the discourses of multicultural education and identity politics with the discourses of critical pedagogy and feminist pedagogy. Viewing multicultural education as a way of teaching more than a curriculum, and as a pedagogy associated with constructivist and postmodern perspectives on knowledge, has had the effect of radically reconstructing the educational process. The new discourse of multicultural education on college campuses still remains somewhat marginalized in academe; but its influence is rising in the 1990s, along with attacks on it from the academic right.

Critical pedagogy as an academic discourse and movement (led by Henry Giroux, Peter McLaren, Ira Shor, and others) began to emerge in the early 1980s and represented, among other things, an effort to move beyond the determinism of neo-Marxist structural and functional models of schooling, with their tendency to treat teachers as agents of domination and to see no room for progressive work in the schools. Gramsci's notion of a "transformative intellectual" or "organic intellectual," a member of the intelligentsia who identifies with movements of liberation and helps articulate their interests and demands, provided one basis for arguing for a new, engaged role for the teacher (Aronowitz & Giroux, 1985). More important, however, the discourse of critical pedagogy began to draw upon the work of Paulo Freire (1970), who developed his "pedagogy of the oppressed" while involved in literacy campaigns to empower Brazilian peasants. Education of the oppressed, Freire argues, must focus on literacy, by which he means learning not merely to read and write, but also to use language in everyday life to produce culture and change the world. In all cases, this calls for dialogue, reflection, and action (praxis). The role of the teacher is to structure dialogue in ways that result in critical self-reflection and praxis.

By the early 1990s, Giroux and McLaren began moving critical pedagogy in a postmodern direction. This has meant several things. First, students are understood to occupy multiple subject positions and be involved in identity formation and struggle along a number of axes of difference, including class, gender, race, and sexual orientation. Second, critical pedagogy is conceptualized as a form of teaching that ruptures or crosses the borders between bipolar oppositional categories of identity. "Border crossing," as Giroux (1992) refers to it, involves respecting and valuing differences among students, but also engaging students in dialogue about "how representations and practices that name, marginalize, and define difference as the devalued Other are actively learned, internalized, challenged, or transformed" (p. 103). Third, the postmodern turn implies a form of pedagogy that explicitly aims at helping students interlink or articulate various struggles over identity around a common or unifying set of democratic principles; and here critical pedagogy has linked up with the notion of a radical democratic "politics of difference."

Over the past few years, a related but somewhat different discourse of feminist pedagogy has emerged in the academy as well. The discourse of feminist pedagogy is generally associated with the shift to a language of "empowerment" that helps students "clarify how relations of domination subordinate subjects marked by gender, ethnicity, class, sexuality, and many other markers of difference" (Luke & Gore, 1992, p. 1). Classroom interaction, in this context, becomes a dialogue in which all "voices" are heard and all "truths" are understood to be partial and contradictory. The objective of classroom discourse is thus not so much to achieve consensus on one "true" or "objective" depiction of social phenomena, or even to come together in support of a unifying "politics of difference," but rather to clarify differences and agreements and work toward coalition building across difference, when possible, to reconstruct power relations (Ellsworth, 1989). This necessitates a language that recognizes the specificity of the Other, a language that facilitates personal sharing and the production of narratives. Finally, feminist pedagogy has emphasized new forms of leadership and authority in the classroom that are based on collaboration, negotiation, and empowering Others rather than having power over them (Blackmore, 1989). Rejecting both a "leading" role for the teacher (leading students toward "truth") and a neutral facilitator role, feminists have been willing to live with the contradictions and ambiguities of supporting democratic beliefs and values in ways that are not coercive or overbearing. Since all individuals are involved in power relations and are influenced by their class, gender, race, and sexual identities, the teacher cannot claim some neutral high ground, removed from the battle, representing the voice of pure "reason." Yet, the teacher also cannot slip into the trap of treating all truths as equal, since some legitimate oppressive practices and others participate in reconstructing power in more equitable and nonoppressive ways. Deborah Britzman (1992) expresses this pedagogic ambiguity nicely: "There is both the hope that students will say what they think and the fear of insensitive thoughts, the desire for students to take up concerns for social justice and the dread that they will hold onto repressive discourses as if they were their own. In such a combination, the boundaries of persuasion—of who persuades whom—blur" (p. 167).

There has been much debate in the academy over the past few years between those associated with critical pedagogy and those associated with feminist pedagogy, much of it acrimonious. However, the differences between these two strands of critical discourse are much inflated. In fact, both are moving in similar directions in the 1990s since both are grounded in poststructural and postmodern perspectives. Together, they provide a working model of a different way of "doing" multicultural education that has important implications for a democratic-progressive discourse on educational renewal. There are, nevertheless, unresolved problems within the discourses of critical pedagogy and feminist pedagogy that need to be resolved in order to more effectively link them to a broad-based movement for change in education. The shift to postmodern theory has been associated with an emphasis on empowerment in terms of various relatively autonomous movements of identity and has not provided much of a basis for integrating identity politics within a broader conception of a democratic community. In fact, without such a conception of identity within a democratic community, the effect of this brand of multicultural education may be to promote bipolar oppositional forms of identity formation and further fragmentation among students. Furthermore, class identity tends to be the one identity *not* associated with identity politics as attention has shifted to race, gender, and sexual identity. This means that while earlier structural, neo-Marxist discourses tended to reduce everything to class, the discourses of critical pedagogy and feminist pedagogy too often have ignored or downplayed the influence of class on identity formation. Still, with all of these caveats, critical and feminist pedagogies offer some sense of what could be in public education and thus some basis for advancing multicultural education "settlements" consistent with democratic projects.

CONCLUSION: MULTICULTURAL EDUCATION IN UNSETTLING TIMES

I have argued that multicultural education may be understood as emerging out of, and related to, broad-based settlements between dominant and oppositional power blocs and social movements. As such it provides one of the primary terrains of struggle over the cultural construction of identity and community. Particularly during the past 2 decades of neoconservatism in U.S. politics and culture, the progressive and democratic potential of multicultural education has been circumscribed or blocked. However, even in conservative times, multicultural education has provided an important space for progressive work in schools, and its contradictions provide an important basis for critiquing what is and envisioning what could be. What directions is multicultural education likely to take in the late 1990s? That, of course, is dependent on which social movements are able to organize a power bloc and discourse on school reform that construct a new hegemonic "common sense." At this point, neoliberalism (constructed primarily around elements of the business community, organized labor, the women's movement, the civil rights movement, and the gay and lesbian rights movement) does not appear to imply a fundamental break with neoconservative educational policy, although it does provide more room for maneuvering. For example, it is at least formally committed to extending equity agendas and building a community of difference, which implies more attention to multicultural education. Neoliberals also appear to be more receptive to extending multicultural education in public schools to include some discussion of gay and lesbian identity and rights. At the same time, the neoliberal power bloc is very fragile and its discourse deeply contradictory. It is heavily driven by economic rationales and agendas that privilege the interests and perspectives of multinational capitalism, yet it does not wish to further alienate labor leadership and rank-and-file workers; and it is committed to extending the agendas of the new identity politics movements of gender, race, and sexuality, while at the same time not encouraging more backlash that plays into the interests of New Right groups.

All of this suggests that the 1990s are a decade marked by an "unsettling" of social and educational policy settlements as conflict intensifies along a number of cultural fronts. Class inequalities continue to widen as we move into a "post-fordist" economy; and a new U.S. underclass is being constructed within inner cities that is increasingly nihilistic, alienated, and prone to express rage through violence, as in the riots that followed the first verdict in the Rodney King beating case in Los Angeles. As African Americans, Latinos/as, women, and gays and lesbians have become more discontented with the lack of substantive progress in overcoming inequities and discriminatory practices over the past few decades, an era of relative quiescence and political stability is giving way to an age of not only "talking back" but "acting up" (hooks, 1989). At the same time that marginalized groups have begun to place increasing pressure on social policy settlements, these settlements face increased pressure from a broad range of New Right groups with their calls for a return to a "common culture" that is unabashedly Eurocentric, patriarchal, and heterosexist. Without the progressive influence of trade unionism, and partially because they face increased job competition from racial minorities and women, white working-class males may be constructing their identities as "other than" female and "other than" Black and thus moving in the political direction of the New Right (Weis, 1990).

Within this volatile cultural and political context, democratic and progressive forces will need to articulate a persuasive new commonsense discourse that is consistent with the changing times in which we live. Throughout this chapter I have speculated on how multicultural education might be reconstructed within such a democratic progressive discourse; I now want to briefly reiterate and elaborate on several of these themes. We must begin, I believe, by affirming a commitment to multicultural education as central to the mission of public education and as integrated throughout the "core" curriculum. We live in increasingly multicultural societies, and the central challenge to democracy in the twenty-first century will be the construction of a community of equity and shared values within a society that is culturally diverse and fragmented by identity and interest groups. The postmodern notion of a "politics of difference" may represent an important step in the formulation of a multicultural education for these new times. The implication is that we view clashes of interests, beliefs, and values among students and school staff as positive, in that they provide a mechanism for hearing all voices, negotiating across difference, and staying responsive to the unique interests and perspectives of all involved parties. A politics of difference also implies offering students and parents more choice among schools, curriculum programs, and approaches to instruction. In business the shift to post-fordist forms of organization, made possible by new computer and information technologies, is allowing for greater client or customer choice, with a decentralization of decision making and production tailored to client specifications. Public school choice programs such as magnet schools are a step in the right direction, although more choices need to be made available and parents, students, and community groups need to be more involved in deciding what is offered. Although I have been critical of the essentialistic tendencies of Afrocentric and feminist discourses, magnet schools based on Afrocentric and feminist curricula certainly would offer some students a chance to affirm who they are within a supportive and nurturing environment; such choices need to be supported. Of course, we also must work to ensure that more choice does not result in more inequality, which surely would be the outcome of an unrestricted voucher system of choice (as proposed by conservatives), and which is already the outcome of a system in which public "magnet" schools serve primarily the middle class.

Ultimately, a democratic progressive resettlement of multicultural education will need to take on the institutional ethos of the school itself—particularly the inner-city school. So long as urban schools are defined primarily as controlling institutions of discipline, punishment, and "normalization"—to use Michel Foucault's (1979) terminology—then we will not be able to get very far in building a truly democratic and multicultural curriculum and pedagogy of empowerment. This is, of course, the dilemma of working within the system to advance democratic projects. Progress must be piecemeal at best, a kind of holding action, until public education can be "reinvented" primarily as an institution of empowerment rather than of socialization and control—an institution that actively intercedes to take the side of disempowered and marginalized students as part of a broader public discourse on equity and the building of a diverse new community for the twenty-first century.

5

The Cultural Politics
of Sexuality Education

ONE OF THE CHARACTERISTICS of the new times we are entering is that struggles over sexuality have moved from the margins to the center of American politics and culture. The AIDS crisis, the abortion issue, the question of adolescent sexuality and contraception, and the emergence of sexual orientation as an axis of struggle—all have provided contexts within which social movements of the left and right have organized to do battle. Just as class, race, and gender have their politics, sexuality has a politics; and that politics is assuming an increasingly central role in American culture. In the 1990s, if one looks for evidence of organized struggle over the public school curriculum, certainly the most visible and publicized struggle is over sexuality education. How should democratic educators respond to the battle being waged over the sexuality curriculum? Is it either possible or desirable to remain neutral in this battle?

In order to address these questions, I want to locate the current battle over sexuality education within the context of an historical battle over sexuality in American culture in this century. For while these are new times, many of the themes that dominate the discourse on sexuality education in the late twentieth century are similar to ones that have been influential throughout the century and are related to deep-rooted cultural theories of sexuality. By "cultural theory of sexuality" I mean to refer here to a commonsense or taken-for-granted set of beliefs about sexuality that are embedded within cultural discourses and practices and that are involved in the control, regulation, and policing of sexual desire—which is also to say, involved in a cultural politics. Often, cultural theories of sexuality are given legitimacy within academic or religious discourse, but I mean to locate their roots deeper within the commonsense beliefs and practices of the broader culture, and link them to particular sets of interests within contemporary culture. Specifically, I want to discuss four cultural theo-

Somewhat modified versions of this chapter were published as "Conflict and Change in the Discourse on Sexuality Education" by D. Carlson, 1991, *Educational Theory, 41*, pp. 343–359; and "Ideological Conflict and Change in the Sexuality Curriculum" by D. Carlson, 1992. In J. Sears (Ed.), *Sexuality and the Curriculum* (pp. 34–58), New York: Teachers College Press.

ries of sexuality: (1) a *repressive* theory that associates sexuality with sin and sickness and emphasizes conformity to narrowly prescribed sexual norms; (2) a *utilitarian progressive* theory of sexual "adjustment" and the management of sexual "problems" to lessen social costs; (3) a *postconventional* theory of liberated sexuality and the politicization of sexuality; and (4) a *libertarian* theory of sexual diversity and individual sexual rights. Obviously, while some of these cultural theories are more democratic than others, I want to suggest that each has something worthwhile to offer in forging a democratic progressive response to the battle over sexuality education. At the same time, democratic progressives will have to take sides in opposing some of the antidemocratic tendencies reflected in the repressive and utilitarian theories in particular.

THE REPRESSIVE THEORY

In the late nineteenth and early twentieth centuries the perspective on sexuality that civic, religious, and educational leaders most uniformly endorsed was what Michel Foucault (1980) called "Victorian puritanism" (p. 22) and what I will refer to as the repressive theory of sexuality. The core values and precepts of this theory were repressive in the sense that they upheld a moralistic conception of sexuality and sin that had deep roots in Judeo-Christian culture, although it was also a modern theory to the extent that it incorporated scientific and economic perspectives in support of sexual puritanism.

The repressive theory was consistent with traditional Judeo-Christian doctrines in several ways. First, it endorsed asceticism, the self-disciplined renunciation of bodily pleasures, which in turn is based on the dichotomization of body and mind, spirit and flesh. While the mind is viewed as important in maintaining the spiritual side of the individual for eternal life, the body is believed to corrupt and tempt the spirit away from its true path (Petras, 1978). Second, traditional Judeo-Christian religious doctrine affirms sexual activity only within the confines of marriage for the purpose of bearing children; and from the restriction against nonprocreative sexuality is derived a long list of prohibitions against "adultery," "sodomy," and homosexuality (Delamater, 1989). Finally, the repressive theory may be related to patriarchal authority structures in various institutions, including the family, the church, and the state. Religious and civic leaders in the Victorian era argued, much as religious traditionalists do today, that the family was being torn apart by "modern" influences that threatened the very foundations of civilization and authority. The situation could be reversed by returning to an idealized patriarchal family grounded on authority and clearly defined roles in which women were to be good mothers, homemakers, and wives, and in all of these roles were to be thoroughly subordinated.

In the early twentieth century, this repressive, religion-based theory of sexuality was still very influential in shaping American culture and was largely taken for granted in the discourse of early sexuality educators, even though the new profession of sexuality education was decidedly secular and modern. As Foucault (1979) suggests, the "expert" has taken on many priestly roles in the modern era, so perhaps it should not be surprising that dominant religious views of sexuality in the culture would find their way into the emerging profession of sexuality education and its crusading spirit. Sigmund Freud's theory was particularly important in this regard, since it translated so many traditional Judeo-Christian beliefs into the new language of science and progress. To Freud, modern industrial civilization was the crowning achievement of human development, made possible because humankind had pulled itself up by its own bootstraps (to borrow the popular metaphor of the age) from the barbarism, chaos, and savagery of the natural or "primitive" world and had accepted the "duty" of responsible labor and the need for legitimate authority. Education, then, was presented as a process of "civilizing little savages," much as European colonialism was understood as part of a benign process of "civilizing" the "primate" peoples of Africa, Asia, and America.

Freudian theory is grounded on the division of the life force into two major principles: the *pleasure principle* and the *reality principle*. Of the former, which is the organizing principle of the young child and "primitive" humankind, Freud (1930/1961b) noted, "It aims, on the one hand, at an absence of pain and unpleasure, and, on the other, at the experiencing of strong feelings of pleasure" (p. 124). All animalistic behavior in the "natural" world thus was explainable as an effort to attain immediate gratification of instinctual desires and/or to avoid unpleasure. In more specifically sexual terms, the pleasure principle was uninhibited by social constraints, which resulted in "polymorphous perversity," an amorphous form of "immature" sexuality in which the individual finds sexual interest in a number of forms and with partners of either or both genders. According to Freud (1920/1961a), the pleasure principle can never achieve its desire fully, and long-term happiness necessitates a good deal of hard work, responsibility, and self-discipline. Thus, he believed that the pleasure principle gradually was replaced in the developing individual, through the processes of informal socialization and formal education, by the reality principle. The reality principle "does not abandon the intention of ultimately obtaining pleasure, but it nevertheless demands and carries into effect the postponement of satisfaction, the abandonment of a number of possibilities of gaining satisfaction and the temporary toleration of unpleasure as a step on the long indirect road to pleasure" (p. 4). In utilitarian terms, the reality principle represents enlightened and long-term self-interest. The "well-adjusted" adult learns how to channel sexuality into socially acceptable outlets (sublimation) and to limit sexual expression to procreation. "Just as a cautious business-man avoids tying up all his capital in one concern," Freud (1930/1961b, p. 33) argued, so the well-adjusted individual learns to avoid investing too heavily in the pleasure principle. Freud thus legitimated a world of instinctual renunciation and compulsory labor not only as an unavoidable necessity but also as a wise personal investment of psychic capital (Cohen, 1982).

Freudian sublimation theory also was used to legitimate the popular "semen theory of power" that was taught to boys in many health education classes through the first half of this century. According to this theory, semen was a major source of nourishment for the mind and body if it was allowed to be reabsorbed by the blood rather than expended or "wasted" in sexual indulgence. Friedrich Nietzche (1954), in seeking to formulate a philosophy of power, observed that "the reabsorption of semen by the blood is the strongest nourishment and, perhaps more than any other factor, it prompts the stimulus of power, the unrest of all forces toward the overcoming of resistance" (p. 75). The influential sexuality educator John Cowan (1874) contended that reabsorbed semen was transformed in the brain into "grand conceptions of the true, the beautiful, the useful, or into fresh emotions of joy and impulses of kindness" (p. 92). Since only men produced semen, this theory legitimized patriarchal power relations at the same time that it legitimized the repression of overt sexuality. Since semen was treated as a commodity of value that needed to be saved and invested wisely rather than squandered or wasted, the semen theory of power took for granted and reinforced the economic rationality of the capitalist world view. As a strong will enabled an individual to ward off the temptations of the flesh, it also enabled the individual to succeed in business (Strong, 1972). The semen theory of power was used by sexuality educators of the early twentieth century to refute another widely held belief of the time—that of "sexual necessity" for adolescent males. Adolescent girls were viewed as less of a "problem" in this regard since they presumably had few sexual feelings (Imber, 1982). They were to learn the importance of "duty" as opposed to personal happiness.

Aside from Freudian theory, early sexuality educators drew upon a scientific-medical theory that linked sin with sickness. Because Victorians associated bodily cleanliness with virtue and moral purity, it was presumed that one could "inoculate" oneself against various diseases and nervous conditions through a strict regimen of bodily hygiene. More specifically, sexual hygiene involved avoiding intimate (or even casual) contact with those who were sexually "unclean" and "diseased." This was considered to be the best prophylactic or preventative measure against contracting sexually transmitted and other degenerative diseases—a message clearly communicated in the title of the nation's first society, organized in 1905, to promote sexuality education in the schools, The American Society of Sanitary and Moral Prophylaxis. The emphasis on sexual hygiene also is revealed in a report from the U.S. Surgeon General and U.S. Bureau of Education (1922) that suggested that high school sexuality education for girls should have as its objectives to make girls more careful about "marrying a man who is free from . . . diseases, to make them more careful as to their choice of friends, and to take precautions in public toilets" (p. 62). A lack of sexual hygiene (including having sex with prostitutes or military men who might be infected with venereal diseases, having sexual relations with "feeble-minded" persons, or even having sex to "excess") was associated with physical and mental degeneracy. Disease, consequently, was depicted as the "wages of sin," much as AIDS has been depicted by New Right fundamentalists in contemporary American society. As Cowan (1874) observed, "The heaven-ordained law to increase and multiply and replenish the earth is being . . . greatly perverted, avoided, broken, and by ways and means that not only prevent the carrying out of the spirit of the command, but, *with a just judgement, bring the perpetrators thereof to a life of bodily sickness [and] mental suffering*" (p. 21; emphasis added). Early sexuality educators argued that most bodily ailments, including "nearly all the inflammatory and chronic diseases that afflict mankind, and especially womankind," were the result of sexual sin and poor sexual hygiene. Among women, "female hysteria," moodiness, and "nervousness" were said to result from a failure in sexual role adjustment. Young people, it was argued, needed education on sexual hygiene because the least educated, rather than being protected and innocent, "are the ones who, through wrong and perverted natures, have committed sexual sins" (p. 22).

The repressive theory had the most influence over the sexuality curriculum in public schools in the first several decades of this century. Its primary sponsors were crusaders, often religiously affiliated, who were fighting a battle against what they saw as a breakdown of moral order that had accompanied urbanization and industrialization. They were effective because they were able to mobilize local support to influence school boards across the country, particularly in small towns and rural areas. The recent resurgence of the repressive theory may be attributed to similar factors. New Right groups have been effective in mobilizing discontent among those who feel, with some justification, that the moral codes that once held the fragile fabric of social life together are collapsing all around them. In the 1980s, New Right groups proved effective in influencing federal educational policy under the Reagan and Bush administrations since they had become such powerful actors in the new Republican party. As a payoff, the U.S. Department of Health and Human Services funded only programs to promote sexual abstinence among teenagers, such as the influential "Sex Respect" program, which emphasize a "just say no" approach to sex with slogans such as, "Pet your dog, not your date" and "Control your urgin', be a virgin" (Flax, 1990). Of course, there is no evidence to suggest that abstinence is (or for that matter ever was) a realistic option for adolescents, or that sexually transmitted diseases can be controlled only through complete abstinence. In the age of AIDS, adolescents are far more likely to be receptive to information on "safe sex'' than no sex; and by continuing to urge them to "just say no" to sex rather than informing them of safe sex practices, an abstinence-only curriculum actually may contribute to the spread of sexually transmitted diseases. Finally, while New Right groups have supported abstinence-only programs in schools, they have preferred that public schools have no programs at all. Silencing is, in the end, the most powerful weapon of repression (Fine, 1988).

There would appear to be little room for common ground between democratic progressivism and a repressive theory of sexuality education. In most cases, democratic progressivim will need to carve out a position on sexuality education that is not only different from, but oppositional to, the repressive theory of the New Right. Nevertheless, I think it unwise to dismiss the concerns and fears raised by the New Right having to do with a breakdown of the family, an erosion of ethics, and a tendency of popular culture to "sell" American youth a narcissistic, self-indulgent representation of self. These problems, however, cannot be solved by returning to an image of an earlier, romanticized past where young people supposedly waited until marriage to have sexual relations, where homosexuality was kept safely locked in the closet, and where there were only two types of girls—"good" girls who were virgins, and "bad" girls who had sex. For this is not only an unreal image, that is, one that does not reflect the reality of our culture, but also an oppressive image to the extent that efforts are made to realize it.

THE UTILITARIAN PROGRESSIVE THEORY

Progressivism, as I indicated in Chapter 1, has been a very broad-based reform movement in education in this century, encompassing diverse strands and tendencies—some of them democratic and some quite authoritarian and elitist. Those progressives who have exercised the most direct influence over the shaping of the sexuality curriculum have tended to believe that education should intervene in society to help overcome or ameliorate certain social "problems" associated with adolescent sexuality (particularly unwanted teenage pregnancies and sexually transmitted diseases). In this sense, they have represented a utilitarian theory of sexuality concerned very pragmatically with the public "costs" of sexual behavior. By the 1920s, this utilitarian theory began to gain wide influence among sexuality educators, and by the 1930s it was the established orthodoxy within the profession. Progressive sexuality educators, most of whom were teachers or counselors in public schools, were proudly secular rather than religious in orientation and they represented modern, rational, scientific approaches to understanding and dealing with social problems. As such, they were more concerned with effectively managing the "problem" of adolescent sexuality than with invoking moralistic arguments against teenage sex. Progressive sexuality educators also were enamored of the idea that the modern state could help solve social problems through rational planning and policy making, an idea they applied to the problems of sexually transmitted diseases, unwanted pregnancies, population control, and the improvement of the genetic stock of the population (racial hygiene or eugenics).

Supporters of a repressive sexuality curriculum had invoked Freudian theory in support of their views, but Freudian theory also provided progressive sexuality educators with a "modern" sexual ethic: one grounded not on repression (at least not exclusively) but rather on sublimation and limited expression, and one more consistent with modern secular than with traditional religious values. In fact, Freud (1930/1961b) had maintained that among the upper-middle-class patients he treated, overrepression and a highly developed superego or sense of guilt were more often the source of various traumas, anxieties, and psychic blockages than was underrepression. In some individuals, this repression was so complete that a productive engagement with life was replaced by "permanent internal unhappiness" (p. 83). Freud thus was led to conclude that "temptations to instinctual satisfaction . . . are merely increased by constant frustration, whereas an occasional satisfaction of them causes them to diminish, at least for the time being" (p. 81). In these ways, Freudian theory gave legitimacy to a sexuality curriculum that, by the 1930s in most school districts, recognized some degree of sexual expression in adolescence as not only natural but healthy—so long as it was kept under careful control and supervision by adults. One influential sexuality education text advocated "partial sublimation" for the average adolescent boy, a form of adjustment in which "the physical manifestations of sex are usually confined to occasional erections and involuntary seminal emissions" (Kirkendall, 1940, p. 30). Masturbation, while never encouraged by progressive educators, was never actively discouraged either so long as it was practiced in moderation.

The pragmatic orientation of progressives also led them to be increasingly supportive of contraceptives and even abortion as weapons in the "war" against teenage pregnancy. They based their argument on two major propositions. First, Malthus's study of populations suggested that war, famine, and pestilence exert negative population control in the absence of positive checks on population, including birth control. Virginia Richmond (1934), an influential sexuality educator, located both abortion and contraceptives within the domain of positive checks on population with deep roots in human culture, as revealed by the new science of anthropology. She noted:

> Many tribes knew no better method [of birth control] than infanticide. . . . There came a time, however, when women learned how to produce abortion. . . . Exceedingly primitive peoples have knowledge of *abortifacients*, agents that produce abortion, of one kind or another. However, contraceptive methods or means of preventing conception are found also in many widely separated primitive tribes. (p. 30)

Second, one result of making abortions illegal and illicit, progressives argued, was that many adolescent girls died unnecessarily each year from complications after attempting to give themselves abortions or after receiving an abortion from an unlicensed doctor. Richmond (1934) reported that in the early 1930s "an appalling number [of deaths] occur each year under circumstances that raise the suspicion of abortion, procured illegally or self-induced. . . . The death rate from abortion appears to be rising rapidly, not only in this country but all over the world, except in Russia where abortion has been legalized" (p. 272). Similarly, she noted, when contraceptives were not widely available and people lacked scientific information on contraceptives, they could be "taken advantage of" by charlatans and could "obtain articles or chemicals often harmful to health and sometimes dangerous" (p. 274). The answer, for the progressives, was a more enlightened approach to sexual problems in society, and more sexuality education in the public schools by specially trained and licensed professionals.

When unwed adolescents did become mothers, Richmond (1934) argued that "social workers and students of society . . . are becoming convinced that in very many cases it is better for both mother and child if the girl does not marry, especially at so early an age" (p. 258). Single mothers were to live at home with their parents until a suitable husband could be found. By the 1950s, and especially in the inner city, such single mothers became wards of the welfare state, under the watchful eye of social workers. Just as getting married at an early age was actively discouraged, even in the case of pregnancy, so the dissolution of overly conflictual marriages was acknowledged as an option. Once more, the early progressives looked to Soviet Russia for leadership and as "a vast social laboratory where all sorts of experiments are being carried out" (p. 266) to better manage human sexuality.

Belief in social utilitarianism and support for state intervention to solve pressing social problems also led some progressive educators to support the then-influential racial "hygiene" or eugenics movement in America. Eugenics, the science of racial improvement through selective breeding, was based on the assumption that the genetically weak and unfit placed a particularly heavy financial burden on society and contributed "weak" or "degenerate" genes to the racial gene pool. According to Richmond (1934), "No one denies the staggering cost to the State of our institutions for the feeble-minded, the insane, and the criminals," which included court and other legal proceeding costs, charitable donations, and the cost of clinical and hospital treatment and supervision, all of which were "supported by the responsible members of society for the benefit of the irresponsible" (p. 277). By 1932, 27 states had enacted eugenics laws requiring that the state certify all marriages to ensure that only genetically "fit" individuals married, and granting the state the right to sterilize individuals identified as idiots, imbeciles, epileptics, feebleminded, insane, and in some cases "moral degenerates" (homosexuals) and "sexual criminals" (child molesters and rapists). Over 10,000 sterilizations eventually were performed. In reporting on this "progress," Richmond argued that it represented just a "drop in the bucket, and that a much more extensive eugenics program will be required." In this regard, she cited the eugenics program just getting under way at that time in Germany, where 400,000 were to be sterilized, and noted that "other nations will watch this program with great interest" (p. 277). This statement reads as sadly ironic and tragically misguided in light of what followed in Germany, and it suggests, once more, that the central weakness of mainstream progressivism was its tendency to support, almost unquestioningly, monumental state initiatives to overcome persistent "social problems" that stand in the way of the New Society.

By the early 1950s progressivism and "life-adjustment" education fell under increasing attack, particularly for their collectivist, authoritarian tendencies. In the era of the Cold War, as Americans celebrated a return to individual competitiveness, professional educators rarely identified themselves as progressives. Nevertheless, the progressive ideology has continued to be very influential in state policy designed to promote "family planning" among the urban poor and in the Third World through an increased reliance on contraceptives and abortion. Among the chief advocates of this perspective since the 1960s have been Planned Parenthood and (internationally) the U.S. Agency for International Development (AID). The latter is perhaps the largest distributor of condoms and other birth control devices in the world and has funded projects to establish abortion clinics in a number of Third World countries since the 1950s. While "family planning" for the urban poor and the Third World may be beneficial to the recipients, and the social burden of providing welfare for the children of the poor is undeniably great, this perspective may be compatible with an implicitly racist and elitist view of society associated with a fear that the poor and nonwhite are out-reproducing the white, middle class.

Today, the utilitarian progressive theory continues to be most influential among professional sexuality educators and liberal policy makers. A good example of mainstream progressive discourse on sexuality education in recent years is provided by the National Research Council report, *Risking the Future: Adolescent Sexuality, Pregnancy and Child Bearing* (1986), which was publicly condemned by Reagan administration officials. The report concluded that the birth control pill was the "safest and most effective" contraceptive for adolescent girls and recommended "aggressive public education to dispel myths about health risks for young women" (quoted in Werner, 1986, p. 1). It also recommended that condom machines be placed in areas where adolescent boys congregate, such as high school restrooms. Finally, it advocated that school-based health clinics be established in high schools to distribute birth control devices and information on birth control to students. The social utilitarianism of the report is evident in its emphasis on the severely limited career opportunities of teenage parents and the economic burden on society of maintaining these families, which the report placed at $16.6 billion in federal outlays for Aid to Dependent Children, Medicaid, and food stamps in 1985 (National Research Council, 1986; Werner, 1986).

I have pointed to some of the limitations of this utilitarian progressive discourse on sexuality education, having to do with its tendency to emphasize state management of sexuality and to be more concerned with social costs than with individual freedom. Still, and particularly when contrasted with the repressive theory of sexuality, utilitarianism has some advantages. It is nonjudgmental, for one thing. Furthermore, the public does have a right to be concerned with the social costs of irresponsible and unethical sexual behavior—especially in a time of the AIDS crisis. This concern can be addressed by providing more information to young people so that they can make responsible choices and engaging them in dialogue on the question of what is responsible sexual behavior. However, I would say that the state does not have a right to actively encourage poor, inner-city young women to have abortions rather than keep their children, or to encourage them to become sterilized. Such policy and practice come too close to the kind of policy and practice advocated by early eugenicists. Rather, the emphasis should be on increasing each girl's sense of choice and control over her life, and on ensuring that adolescent mothers and their children are connected with a support network to get the kinds of assistance they need. Admittedly, the attempt to balance social costs and individual rights and freedoms is not always easy. A democratic progressive discourse on sexuality education will need to be forged out of the tension between the two.

THE POSTCONVENTIONAL THEORY

So far I have discussed two theories of sexuality that have exercised a major influence, and increasingly an oppositional influence, over the sexuality curriculum in public schools in the United States. Other, less conventional theories of sexuality also have had some impact, particularly in sexuality education at the postsecondary level. The first of these I want to refer to as the postconventional theory of sexuality. As with other cultural theories of sexuality, some version of postconventional theory is to be found in Freud, and I want to focus my comments here on two of the more influential postconventional interpreters of Freud's work: Wilhelm Reich, who founded the "sexual politics" movement in Germany in the 1920s, and Herbert Marcuse, whose *Eros and Civilization* (1966) influenced the counterculture and sexual liberation movements of the 1960s and 1970s.

In his practice as a psychoanalyst treating both working-class and middle-class patients, Reich (1931/1971) was led to conclude, consistent with Freud, that many individuals were "infected with sexual and neurotic disturbances" (p. xviii) related to an overly rigid adherence to conventional morality. Reich concluded that the working-class patients he treated were just as inhibited, or more so, as the middle-class patients Freud analyzed. As a Marxist, however, Reich proposed a new answer to Freud's famous question, "What interest has society in sexual repression?" His answer was that "morality is a social product that rises and then passes away, and in the class state it is in the service of the ruling class" (p. xvi). Reich argued that the ruling class maintains its control of the working class at least partially through sexual repression. This occurs, he believed, in two interrelated ways. First, control is maintained by channeling or sublimating sexual energy into the political realm, where it supports relations of political domination and subordination, a type of national sadomasochism. Fascism appeals to and molds a particular "character structure" within a population that is based on repressed sexuality and manifested in relations of domination and subordination in various institutional spheres. Second, by recreating in the traditional nuclear family the basic relations of class society, relations of domination and subordination are learned in the home before they become politicized. Here Reich quoted Friedrich Engels's *The Origin of the Family*, which maintained that "in the individual family . . . we have a miniature picture of the same conflicts and contradictions in which society, split into classes since the beginnings of civilization, has been moving, unable to solve or overcome them" (p. 146). Reich (1931/1971) concluded that the "natural morality" of the primitive matriarchal clans, in which people had "sexual freedom based on gratification" (pp. 146–147) was infinitely superior to the repressive patriarchy of industrial capitalism. Compulsory monogamy and patriarchal rule had risen out of and encouraged the concentration of wealth in the hands of a few rich men and was consistent with the development of an authoritarian rather than a self-governing or democratic character structure. To achieve socialism, this character structure had to change; sexuality had to become less repressed and more egalitarian (in Reich's view the two went together).

The implications of this radical politicization of sexual repression by Reich were worked out in the controversial "Sex-Pol" movement, which brought sexual education and a new sexual ideology to the working class of Germany in the 1920s and early 1930s (Cohen, 1982). Reich (1931/1971) sought to encourage among the German working class many of the ideals of the revolutionary sexuality education then officially supported in Soviet Russia, including an acceptance of adolescent sexuality, nonmonogamous relationships, and bearing children out of wedlock. After a visit to Russia in the late 1920s, for example, he observed that "the question whether one wanted to become a sexual partner was being asked more and more openly and unhesitatingly. . . . An acquaintance was in the eighth month of pregnancy, but nobody had asked who the child's father was. A family offered to put up a visitor but didn't have enough room, so the sixteen-year-old daughter said openly to her parents: 'I'll go sleep with X [her boyfriend]'" (pp. xxiii–xxiv). In Soviet schools adolescents were informed openly about procreation, birth, contraception, and venereal disease. Abortions were available and encouraged, and prostitution was largely eliminated. Women were depicted as equals of men in the household and the economy, traditional patriarchal practices were criticized, and permissive or self-regulating patterns of child rearing were encouraged (Cohen, 1982). The official Soviet position on homosexuality was also "modern" and rather tolerant, at least in the beginning under Lenin. All of this official ideology of sexuality in the Soviet Union found its way into the Sex-Pol movement in Germany, although Reich went beyond the official Communist party line in calling for a revolutionary form of working-class desublimation of sexuality, with an emphasis on "genital gratification" rather than reproduction, and the Communist party of Germany ultimately disassociated itself from Reich's views and withdrew its support of the Sex-Pol movement. Reich also became increasingly disenchanted with the Soviets as, under the influence of Stalinism, they became more traditional and repressive in their views on sexuality. For example, in 1934 the official Soviet party line was changed so that homosexuality was viewed as a "sign of a degenerate culture of the perverse bourgeoisie" and a "social crime." The widespread persecution of homosexuals began in January 1934, with mass arrests in the major cities of Soviet Russia. Homosexuals joined other "counterrevolutionary" groups in the rapidly expanding gulags of the Stalinist era, and many died there (Reich, 1945).

Reich provides the basis for one particular form of radical sexual politics. However, Reich still places sexuality at the service of the revolution and the socialist state, and to this extent he developed a radical utilitarian theory of sexuality. The "good" worker and party member is to be forged by encouraging a rejection of bourgeois sexual mores regarding monogamy and other forms of sexual "ownership" and by encouraging gender equality in sexual relations and family life. Reich finally broke with the official Communist party line, but his perspective is still one of sexual uniformity and "politically correct" sexuality. In America, the notion of a politically correct sexuality also has had its appeal among some on the political left, even if what is taken for politically correct sexuality has changed with time.

If Reich represents a particular strand of doctrinaire thinking among the Old Left, then Marcuse represents a quite different strand, more attuned to the American counterculture and New Left of the 1960s and early 1970s. In *Eros and Civilization* (1966), Marcuse took up Freud's questions regarding civilization and its discontents once more, suggesting that Freud actually laid the basis for a society in which the pleasure principle would not need to be repressed.

In very basic terms, he argued that while a good deal of repression and sublimation was necessary to build "civilization" to its current advanced level, it was wrong to suppose that civilization would always require subordination of the pleasure principle to the reality principle, or that a dichotomization of these two principles was necessary. Instead, "the very achievements of repressive civilization seem to create the preconditions for the gradual abolition of repression" (p. 5). Such a change in society need not imply a relapse into barbarism, as Freud feared, since "occurring at the height of civilization, as a consequence not of defeat but of victory in the struggle for existence, and supported by a free society, such liberation might have very different results. It would still be a reversal of the process of civilization, a subversion of culture—but *after* culture had done its work and created the mankind and the world that could be free" (p. 198).

What Marcuse is suggesting here is a restatement of the Marxist notion that alienated labor is not the inevitable lot of humankind, that once the technological means of production and methods of distribution of goods in a society reach a certain point of development (as Marcuse believed they had by the mid-twentieth century), humankind as a whole has the capacity to meet its basic material needs without imposing on individuals the necessity of a life of alienated labor and repression. For the first time, according to Marcuse, humankind was in a position to reap the fruits of thousands of years of labor. Computers and automated production processes could replace much of the drudgery of alienated, routinized labor and allow for more free time for leisure and creative pursuits. The body, no longer used as an instrument of alienated labor, would be resexualized, accompanied by "a reactivation of all erotogenic zones and, consequently, in a resurgence of pregenital polymorphous sexuality and in a decline of genital supremacy. The body in its entirety would become an object of cathexis, a thing to be enjoyed—an instrument of pleasure" (p. 201). There are echoes here of the *Kama Sutra* intertwined with Freudian analysis in support of a return to a more "infantile" (as Freud would say) and generalized sexuality that is not primarily genital intercourse or orgasm oriented—"the primacy of the genital function is broken" (p. 205). Thus, while Reich viewed genital sexuality as the goal in rebellion against bourgeois inhibitions, Marcuse recognized genital sexuality as repressive as well, since it narrowed and constrained sexual expression. Instead of viewing a reactivation of prehistoric and childhood sexual desires as a regression (as Freud had), Marcuse argued that "it may well be the opposite" (pp. 202–203) since it would free up long-repressed potential and desire. Even sadomasochistic sexuality, he argued, is part of our polymorphous perversity, our instinctual being, and when expressed in a free and consensual manner it cannot be equated with the activities of SS Troops. Along with a general reactivation of instinctual sexuality, Marcuse believed that in a nonrepressive society there would be "an enlargement of the meaning of sexuality itself'' involving a resurgence in the creativity of work and all spheres of human activity. Work itself would become "libidinal and erotic" (p. 208) since it would be expressive and creative. In Marxist terms, the freeing of the pleasure principle thus is associated with a return to nonalienated labor. This is, in fact, a sublimation theory of sorts, but one that no longer distinguishes between work and play, between the reality principle and the pleasure principle.

As I noted earlier, Marcuse's model of a liberated sexuality is consistent with the values of the countercultural movement of the 1960s, which challenged the thinking of previous generations on sexuality and the "good life." Salvation was to come not through hard work and self-discipline but through a recapturing of pleasure and love (in all its forms). The traditional family and hierarchical institutional structures at all levels that supported the repressive society were resisted as people experimented with alternative institutional structures. While Marcuse believed that the liberation of eros did not threaten civilization as such, the countercultural movement clearly did threaten hierarchical institutional structures in advanced capitalist America, and its more extreme manifestations had been suppressed rather forcefully by the mid-1970s. In its more mainstream form, the emphasis on the pursuit of pleasure proved to be containable and even exploitable within the consumer society. Still, the postconventional theory of sexuality provides an important critique of contemporary Western culture, and the call for moving beyond its repressive and oppressive values is likely to have continuing relevance in the decades ahead. In fact, some variation of this post-conventional theory of sexuality seems most consistent with democratic progressive values and agendas.

THE LIBERTARIAN THEORY

The final cultural theory of sexuality I want to examine is perhaps particularly American and in some ways quite radical, although not explicitly so. Its radicalness lies, rather, in a "freeing" of sexuality from social utilitarianism and in a championing of individual sexual rights—themes that are becoming increasingly influential in postmodern culture. In choosing to label this theory libertarian, I imply several things. First, "libertarian" implies a *libertine* perspective that proudly celebrates sexuality and sexual diversity in defiance of established mores. Second, it implies *political libertarianism*, the objective of which is to maximize the freedom of individuals to live their lives according to their own values. The only ethical codes accepted within libertarian theory are those of *reciprocity* (I must grant you the same freedom of choice you grant me) and *consensuality* (individuals must enter into relations as consenting adults who mutually agree on the terms of their relationships). Alfred Kinsey, perhaps the most influential sexuality researcher in this century, provides a good example of someone whose work was influenced primarily by a libertarian theory of sexuality. As for regulating sexual expression, he maintained that society properly should "attempt to control sexual relations which are secured through the use of force or undue intimidation," but should otherwise interfere as little as possible in the affairs of individuals (Kinsey, 1953, p. 476).

Kinsey was a statistician and taxonomist of sexuality rather than a theoretician of sexual politics. Yet his treatment of sexuality is likely to shock many conventional readers, even today. As Paul Robinson (1976) points out, Kinsey "is this century's foremost sexual demystifier. . . . [Not] only did Kinsey lack Freud's sense of the demonic element in human sexuality, he was also as untainted by romanticism as any major sexual theorist. . . . [His research] effected a kind of democratization of human sexual affairs. It brought the most tabooed activities under the same conceptual roof as marital relations and in the process rendered them innocuous" (p. 118). The two most influential volumes to come out of Kinsey's Institute for Sexual Research at Indiana University are *Sexual Behavior in the Human Male* (1948) and *Sexual Behavior in the Human Female* (1953). Together, these studies provide the best statistical evidence available, even 4 decades later, on the sexual activities of a broad cross-section of Americans—a tribute to the mass of data Kinsey and his colleagues were able to collect and the sophisticated statistical methods used to ensure that a representative sample was obtained.

Perhaps the most striking and consistent picture that emerges from these studies is of a wide range of "normal" sexual adjustment. First, there was wide variability in normal sexual drive and output among individuals. Kinsey observed, for example, that one male in his study could recall only one orgasm in 30 years, while another male recorded as many as 30 orgasms in 1 week. Second, and more significant, there was wide variability in sexual response or behavior. Kinsey documented six forms of sexual response among men and women (masturbation, nocturnal emissions or sexual dreams, heterosexual petting, heterosexual intercourse, homosexual relations, and bestiality). All of these alternative responses were treated more or less equally, although not all were equally prevalent in the population. What made all sexual responses equal to Kinsey was that each resulted, or could result, in a common physiological response: sexual "output" or orgasm. Kinsey did not, in this regard, distinguish one orgasm from another; all were treated as equal units of sexual outlet. For that matter, male and female orgasms could not be clearly distinguished, he argued, since "all orgasms appear to be physiologically similar quantities, whether they are derived from masturbation, heterosexual, homosexual, or other sorts of activities" (Kinsey, 1953, p. 511).

Probably the most common form of sexual outlet among both men and women, according to Kinsey, was masturbation. Although females seemed to indulge in masturbation less than males, Kinsey (1953) reported that of every possible type of sexual activity, "masturbation . . . is the one in which the female most frequently reaches orgasm" (p. 132). Heterosexual intercourse thus was dethroned as the most erotic or even preferred form of sexual behavior. Kinsey indicated that masturbation was pervasive, harmless, and perhaps even therapeutic, and rejected the psychoanalytic view that it indicated psychic immaturity. According to Kinsey (1953), "We may assert that we have recognized exceedingly few cases, if indeed there have been any outside of a few psychotics, in which either physical or mental damage has resulted from masturbatory activity" (p. 167). In this one sentence, Kinsey demolished the rationale that sexuality educators had used for decades in arguing against masturbation as an "unhealthy habit," and implicitly challenged the whole notion of sublimation, the cornerstone of both traditional and progressive ideologies.

Many viewed Kinsey as a sexual egalitarian, and in some important ways he was. For example, he argued that sexual response was similar in both men and women, thus countering the prevalent notion that women did not experience sexual feeling as much as men did. Furthermore, in viewing the clitoris rather than the vagina as the focus of female sexual arousal and in arguing that the clitoris was most fully stimulated in masturbation, Kinsey encouraged a view of women as more than the passive receptacles of the male sexual organ. In spite of this, Kinsey was not yet a feminist and took for granted a male-centered perspective on human sexuality. For example, he concluded that "in most mammals the behavior of the female in a heterosexual performance usually involves the acceptance of the male which is trying to make intromission. The female at such a moment is less aggressive than the male, even passive in her acceptance of the male's approaches, and subordinate in position to him. . . . There is no sexual relation until the female has been sufficiently subdued to allow the male to effect coitus" (Kinsey, Pomeroy, & Martin, 1948, p. 613). Kinsey's male-centered perspective is evident also in his contention that while women have orgasms, they are less frequent than men's and less important in overall female sexual response. In supporting this notion, Kinsey (1953) argues that "outside of the human species, orgasm is infrequent and possibly absent among females of most species of mammals" (p. 135)—a highly dubious proposition based on little scientific data. Furthermore, the reduction of sexual relations to the achievement of sexual "outlet" takes for granted a particularly masculinist view of sexuality, with attention focused on the most efficient and direct means of achieving orgasm.

Because Kinsey equated sexuality with orgasms, he tended to valorize adolescent males as the top sexual athletes in society, based on their orgasmic "output." In doing so, he also perpetuated many stereotypes that associated masculinity with sexual performance. For example, Kinsey (Kinsey, Pomeroy, & Martin, 1948) argued that those boys who reach puberty earliest also have the highest sex drive in adolescence, and they continue to outperform other males throughout their active sex lives. Kinsey clearly regarded them as superior both physically and socially to boys who reach puberty later. He remarked, for example, that "these early-adolescent males are more often the more alert, energetic, vivacious, spontaneous, physically active, socially extrovert, and/or aggressive individuals in the population," while late-blooming boys have a diminished sexual output and are more typically "slow, quiet, mild in manner, [and] without force" (p. 325). Kinsey thus affirmed the conventional patriarchal wisdom in American society that "masculinity" is unequally distributed, that some men have more than others, and that those who have the most are naturally superior.

While Kinsey represented a particularly male-centric libertarianism, a somewhat different libertarian theory of sexuality is represented in the more recent and widely publicized research by William Masters and Virginia Johnson. Their work may be viewed as expressive of a more balanced or even feminist libertarianism, more consistent with the changing times. Masters and Johnson are best known for *Human Sexual Response* (1966) and *Human Sexual Inadequacy* (1970), two studies designed, either directly or indirectly, to help married couples lead happier sex lives with fewer sexual "dysfunctions" or "disorders" (Lehrman, 1970; Robinson, 1976, Chapter 3). Both of these books reflected and contributed to increased role equalization within the middle-class, college-educated group that Masters and Johnson studied. In a number of ways, women were even depicted as sexually superior to men. They can, for example, achieve multiple orgasms, stay sexually aroused longer, and seem more inclined to enjoy a variety of amorphous response patterns in comparison to men, who are more genital and orgasm oriented.

While Masters and Johnson's concern with sexual adjustment links them to the psychoanalytic tradition, they understood "proper" adjustment (at least within marriage) in a very libertarian way. In the modern marriage, they argued, success is to be measured at least partially by whether or not both partners' sexual desires are met. Marriage is like a sexual contract between consenting heterosexual adults, and like all contracts it must be to the advantage of both parties. With many couples, especially the most dysfunctional ones, one or both partners are not getting their sexual needs met—most typically the woman. Masters and Johnson treated sexual dysfunctions as a component of the overall relationship: If a husband is impotent or a wife unresponsive, the other partner is very much involved both in the cause of the problem and in its treatment. The goal of therapy, consequently, is to open up sexual communication channels between partners so that they can make their needs better known and to provide couples with factual information on how to increase and maintain sexual arousal. Each partner is treated as an equal, and as such is made responsible for ensuring that his or her sexual needs are met, along with the sexual needs of the partner, through open verbal communication of desires and through the use of "body language" (by guiding the hands of the partner, and so forth). Rather than striving to achieve orgasms, both partners are encouraged to explore sensory pleasures. In all of these ways, partners in stable, long-term relationships are encouraged to desublimate in order to increase their sexual utility function, get more out of their relationships, and ensure that their relationships hold together and grow. Sexual relations and problems, following a libertarian logic, are of vital concern to the involved parties but not to the larger society or state.

The libertarian theory of sexuality began to influence the sexuality curriculum in some limited ways by the 1960s, at least in many college-level courses on human sexuality and sexual relations. At the college level, educators feel freer than they do in public school classrooms to speak of sexual desire and fulfillment in positive terms and to emphasize the "open" negotiation of sexual roles and relations. For example, in one popular college text an entire chapter is devoted to the topic of "negotiating relationships." The authors claim that "developing a sexual relationship and keeping it alive and healthy usually involves continuing sensitive negotiation. . . . To get together sexually with another person, we need to understand not only our own ideas about what sex means but theirs, too" (Nass & Fisher, 1988, p. 112). Another college text makes the case for sexual diversity rather than homogeneity in concluding that "the 'traditional' pattern of American family and marriage and the 'traditional' American sexual value system are mythic concepts with no reality because we can see a wide variety of lifestyles and sexual values documented in any serious history of American culture" (Francoeur, 1982, p. 42).

Most of the tenets of the libertarian theory of sexuality are consistent, I believe, with democratic progressive values having to do with increasing human freedom and the establishment of relations of reciprocity and mutual respect. The emphasis on individual sexual rights, including the right to control one's body, is important in the women's and gay and lesbian movements; and the protection of sexual rights, including the rights of sexual minorities, should be a central focus in any democratic progressive discourse on sexuality education. Of course, in public education we are not dealing with adults, and many people believe that sexual "rights" may be fine for consenting adults but are inappropriate for adolescents. However, I think a democratic progressive discourse on sexuality education must begin by affirming that adolescents have sexual desires and that they have certain sexual rights—such as the right to engage in sexual relations with other adolescents, including homosexual relations. Gay adolescents, after all, have a right to sexual lives as much as heterosexual adolescents. In recent years support for adolescent sexual rights has grown among some scholars, and the debate on this issue is likely to become more heated in the years ahead (Rodman, Lewis, & Griffith, 1984). The problem with the libertarian theory of sexuality, from a democratic perspective, is that a focus on individual rights is not enough and may even deflect attention away from the need to struggle on broader cultural fronts. What libertarianism lacks is theory or discourse that links power relations organized and constituted around sexuality with a more general and inclusive theory of power relations in the culture.

CONCLUSION: SEXUALITY EDUCATION AND CULTURAL STUDIES

In my work in public schools, I have heard some educators argue that the public schools should stay out of the conflict brewing over sexuality education as much as possible by teaching students the "facts" about human sexuality and leaving the teaching of values to the family and church. At this point, I hope the folly of such a position is apparent. Since all "facts" are socially constructed and take on meaning only within the context of an explicit or implicit theory about culture, the relevant questions become, Whose facts do we present, and Within the context of which cultural theory of sexuality? The point here is that it is impossible for public education to construct a position of neutrality within the struggle being waged over sexuality in the culture. A democratic progressive sexuality curriculum will need to take sides in support of gay rights, abortion rights, contraception rights, and other rights that return power to individuals to control their own bodies and desires. This need not mean condoning "irresponsible" (i.e., unsafe, obsessive, or unethical) sexual behavior, but only by engaging in a frank, open dialogue on sexuality and sexual identity, can students learn to use their sexual rights responsibly.

One way to encourage such a dialogue is to present students with various cultural theories of sexuality, such as those I have constructed in this chapter, and ask them to explore the implications of the theories. What values do they represent? Whose voices get heard and whose silenced? How do the theories support various power relations of equality or inequality? This moves sexuality education decisively into the realm of cultural studies, that new, postmodern, hybrid discourse that is challenging many of the traditional ways we understand subjects and disciplines in education (Giroux, 1994). Sexuality education certainly should include some instruction in the biological aspects of human sexuality and reproduction. It also needs to include some study of sexual hygiene, that is, sexually transmitted diseases, contraceptive methods, and so forth. These traditional concerns of sexuality educators, however, are only part of the study of human sexuality. A cultural studies perspective reminds us that sexuality is something that is produced and given meaning within cultural and historical contexts (Foucault, 1980). This implies several things. First, sexuality education would focus on issues of difference and diversity among cultures. That is, it would seek to understand how different cultures name and give meaning to sexuality. Second, a cultural studies focus implies recognizing differences within a given culture. Thus, we are encouraged to raise issues having to do with the different ways in which sexuality is related to race, class, gender, and other identities. Third, cultural studies imply an historical perspective. Students need to recognize that contemporary values and beliefs about sexuality are not the same for all time. Rather, sexual power relations have a dynamic, unresolved quality, have changed substantially over time, and are now in the process of changing. Finally, a cultural studies focus encourages us to view sexuality as implicated in power relations and cultural struggle. All of these must be important components of a democratic progressive approach to sexuality education, which suggests that the field will need to be reconceptualized considerably before we can begin to make much progress.

6

Gayness, Multicultural Education, and Community

WHILE PUBLIC SCHOOLS have long been viewed by progressive educators as embryonic communities that should engage young people in building a democratic community of mutual support and respect, gay people for the most part have been made absent, invisible, and silent within this community and at the same time represented as the deviant and pathological Other. In what follows, I not only want to point to some of the ways gay people and "gayness" have been "kept in their place" in the school community, but, more important, I want to argue that these practices are increasingly hard to sustain. Public schools are being drawn into the battle brewing between "New Right" fundamentalists and progressives in American culture as older forms of community and family are beginning to disappear and cultural diversity is increasing. Within this unsettling context, I want to suggest that public schools may play an important role in helping to build a new democratic, multicultural community, one in which sexual identity (like other markers of difference, including class, gender, and race) is recognized, in which inequities are challenged, and in which dialogue across difference replaces silencing and invisibility practices (Burbules & Rice, 1991).

Throughout much of this century, the dominant idea of community in America was represented by what I will call the *normalizing community*. Within normalizing communities, some individuals and subject positions (i.e., white, middle class, male, heterosexual, etc.) are privileged and represented as "normal," while other individuals and subject positions (i.e., Black, working class, female, homosexual, etc.) are disempowered and represented as deviant, sick, neurotic, criminal, lazy, lacking in intelligence, and in other ways "abnormal." Public schools in particular often have promoted such "normalizing" conceptualizations of community that are based on defining a cultural center or "norm" and positioning class, gender, race, and sexual Others at the margins. In particular, marginalization may be associated with tracking and ability-grouping prac-

A slightly revised version of this chapter was originally published as "Gayness, Multicultural Education, and Community" by D. Carlson, 1994, *Educational Foundations, 8*(4), pp. 5–26.

tices, with "deficit" theories of the child and his or her family, and with curriculum practices that exclude the contributions and voices of various Others. However, as those marginalized within this normalizing discourse on community have begun to speak out and challenge their marginalization, and also have begun to develop collective movements and communities of support, the modernist idea of homogeneous, normalizing community is being more seriously disrupted than ever before.

In the struggle brewing in American culture over the reconstruction of community, three divergent perspectives have emerged. The first of these may be associated with the notion of a "community of interest." As the idea of a cohesive, monolithic community is collapsing, new social movements of identity are forming their own, relatively autonomous communities, speaking their own discourses. I see some merit to this idea of community although I also believe it is fundamentally limited. It has helped marginalized groups find their own voices and create spaces of their own; and it seems to me consistent with the extension of human freedom and the renewed emphasis on identity in the postmodern era. This comes at a cost, however. Community is redefined in a noninclusive manner so that we are unable to articulate a common or "public" interest.

A second emergent discourse on community in America is that associated with the New Right and cultural neoconservatism. This is a discourse about recapturing a romanticized lost American community, a "Father Knows Best" community where authority is respected, everybody "knows their places," and culture is homogenous. It is also a community with a less benign face, one that maintains a dominant culture through oppressive tactics used to keep Others "in their places." Arthur and Marilouise Kroker (1993) refer to this as a community organized around the "will to purity," involving a "vengeance-seeking search for scapegoats on whom expiation can be found for the absence at the center of society . . . and a panic fear of viral contamination by swirling impurities: exchanges of bodily fluids, transgressionary thoughts, women rebelling against the sovereignty of lines" (p. 3). In unsettling times, such hyper-normalizing constructions of community have a wide, popular appeal.

Yet a third discourse on community to emerge over the past decade or so in America is associated with the notion of a community of difference and diversity—what I will call a democratic multicultural community. Within this discourse, community is redefined so that difference is recognized outside of binary oppositions, space is provided for identity groups to form their own communities of interest, and at the same time a common, public culture is continuously being constructed and reconstructed through dialogue across difference (Tierney, 1993). Despite all of the unresolved tensions presented by this reconceptualization of community, I think it may serve as a useful framework for articulating a new progressive agenda for educational renewal, one organized around the process of "becoming somebody" in a democratic multicultural community (Wexler, 1993).

Before proceeding, it seems important that I say something more about my use of the terms *gay* and *gayness* in this chapter. The commonsense perspective on language is that words refer to or stand for things, so that it does not really matter what you call these things. However, words do not merely stand in for "things." They emerge out of and take on meaning within particular discourses and practices. Thus, the words *homosexual, gay, lesbian*, and *queer* have histories we have to consider when we invoke them. Homosexual is an ostensibly neutral category, one designed by scientists; and yet its usage may involve a scientific distancing from the homosexual object of study and a refusal to see the political and cultural elements of sexual identity. Gay and lesbian or gay men and lesbians are the most "politically correct" labels, although their usage tends to further divide and separate men and women when in fact homophobia and oppression are directed against homosexuals as a group. I thus rely most frequently on the term *gay* to refer to both men and women in a way that has become common in popular culture. Of course, this term, to the extent that it invokes a bipolar construct of "straight/gay," may serve to police its own boundaries and set up its own oppositions. Queer recently has become reappropriated from its oppressive context of usage to support a militant form of standing outside of conventional roles, and its use is creeping into gay culture generally and into gay studies in the academy (Corey, 1993; Leck, 1993–94). Yet, "queerness" represents a celebration of the outsider that may not link up effectively with a democratic-progressive politics of inclusion. Finally, I want to distinguish between a homosexual orientation or preference and gay identity. The former I take to refer to the more-or-less natural direction of one's sexual desires, while the latter refers to the active construction of a gay self-identity and visible gay presence within culture—what I am referring to as gayness.

THE NORMALIZING SCHOOL COMMUNITY AND GAYNESS

I want to begin by mapping out in more specificity some of the ways in which gayness has been marginalized within the modern, normalizing school community that has predominated throughout much of the twentieth century in America. Since all normalizing communities maintain a center and margins in the face of opposition and resistance from those being marginalized, analysis needs to proceed through an account of the specific techniques and apparatuses of power that have been employed in the school to keep gayness "in its place" as an invisible presence. Three techniques of normalization and (hence) marginalization have been of primary importance in this regard: (1) the erasure of gayness in the curriculum, (2) the "closeting" and "witch-hunting" of gay teachers, and (3) verbal and physical intimidation of gay teachers and students.

One way that a normalizing curriculum or text works is by presenting students with a "selective tradition" (Williams, 1989). To some degree, all traditions of culture and knowledge, even multicultural traditions, must be selective, for the production of a text always involves a selection process in which something must be left out. Nevertheless, normalizing texts systematically exclude and neglect the culture of those outside the norm for the purpose of ratifying or legitimating the dominant culture as the only significant culture worth studying. This exclusionary aspect of the construction of a selective tradition is particularly important in understanding how texts have worked with regard to gayness. For we do not get very far if we we look for what *is* said about gayness in educational texts. We get much farther if we pay attention to what Susan Sellers (1991) calls the "silent spaces" or the "not said" of the text, and what Mike Cormack (1992) and others have called the "structuring silences" within texts. Not only do these silent spaces work to make those on the margins invisible and silent; they also, and at the same time, make the cultural center invisible as a center since it never has to "speak its own name" (Ferguson, 1990).

At the level of state educational policy, it is noteworthy that no state currently recognizes gays and lesbians as legitimate minority or cultural groups to be considered in textbook adoption or to be included in multicultural education; and a number of states explicitly prohibit teaching about homosexuality. In 1993, for example, the gay rights movement claimed a major victory in the signing into law of a Minnesota bill that makes it illegal to discriminate against lesbians and gay men in employment and housing. Yet, what was ignored in all the celebrating was a provision in the bill that prohibits teaching about homosexuality in the public schools (Kielwasser & Wolf, 1993–94). In such an environment, it hardly should be surprising that major textbook publishers avoid gayness like the plague. English literature anthologies still go out of their way to avoid acknowledging that certain famous writers were gay, such as Gertrude Stein, Walt Whitman, or James Baldwin. This cleansing of gayness from the literary canon often is defended as an effort to maintain the reputation or "good name" of authors by not "outing" them. Yet such concern is, of course, another way of affirming that being gay is cause for a loss of respect. Aside from being a visible absence in the curriculum, gayness has been made visible in some limited and marginalized contexts. To the extent that gayness is recognized in the curriculum, it is likely to be in the health curriculum, where it is associated with disease. For example, one of the most popular health texts on the high school market is *Health: A Guide to Wellness*, which mentions homosexuals or homosexuality once in acknowledging that "the first group in the United States diagnosed with AIDS were male homosexuals" (quoted in Kielwasser & Wolf, 1993–94, p. 64).

Normalizing practices, however, must reach beyond curriculum texts if they are to be effective in constructing a normalizing school community. Throughout this century, one of the primary means of ensuring that gayness was an invisible presence in the school was through the dismissal of teachers who were found out to be homosexuals. Early in the century, the dismissal of gay teachers was legitimated as a way of keeping young people from being exposed to improper role models, lechery, and child molestation. Willard Waller, in his influential book, *The Sociology of Teaching* (1932), argued that homosexuals should not be allowed to teach for two primary reasons. First, employing a disease metaphor, he argued that homosexual teachers represented a danger to their students since "nothing seems more certain than that homosexuality is contagious" (pp. 147–148). Much as communist teachers were to be drummed out of the teaching corps because communism was "contagious," so gay teachers were to be fired because they too were understood as contagious—and in the height of the McCarthy era in the late 1940s and early 1950s, homosexuality and communism were closely linked as threats to the "American way of life." In both cases, the association with sickness and disease provided a means of legitimating isolation from impressionable young people. Second, homosexual teachers were presumed to be lecherous and to develop "ridiculous crushes" on students. Waller observed, "The homosexual teacher develops an indelicate soppiness in his relations with his [sic] favorites . . . and makes minor tragedies of little incidents when the recipient of his attentions shows himself indifferent." Waller went on to suggest that because homosexual teachers were always victims of such "crushes," this was inevitably "fatal to school discipline" (p. 148). Since homosexuals were therefore ineffective as teachers, Waller encouraged administrators to be on the lookout for "latent homosexuals" when they were hiring teachers. Among the best indications of homosexuality, according to Waller, were "such personality traits as carriage, mannerisms, voice, speech, etc." (p. 148). Waller thus provides a good example of how "expert" knowledge on homosexuality as a pathological disorder was used to legitimate "witch-hunts" in the schools for homosexual teachers. Today, witch-hunts against gay teachers are (for the most part) a thing of the past, and many lesbian and gay male teachers are relatively "out" among a select group of co-workers. Yet the intimidation continues, much as it does in the military. The official policy in most school districts is in fact identical to that of the U.S. military, namely, "don't ask, don't tell." Interestingly, while this policy is being challenged by gays in the military, it has not been challenged forcefully by gay teachers in public schools yet, perhaps because they feel (probably rightly so) they could not win if they pushed their case.

One of the effects of this closeting of gay teachers may be an overzealous effort by gay teachers themselves to avoid any class discussion in which gayness may come up, since they presume that to be publicly "out" at school would cost them their jobs. In *Growing Up Gay in the South* (1991), which weaves together the narratives of 36 southern lesbians and gay men coming of age in the 1970s and 1980s, James Sears reports a case of a gay high school English teacher who went out of his way in introducing Walt Whitman's poetry to avoid discussing recent scholarly interpretations of the work that emphasize its homoerotic themes. The teacher remarked, "There is a kind of terror that runs through my mind when I think about that [mentioning gay themes in Whitman's poetry]. There's a Pandora's Box that's opened with that. . . . I just don't know if students are mature enough or whether that's a subject that in this environment we can deal with" (p. 399). In this case, the fear is not only of acknowledging Whitman's sexual identity, but of having to acknowledge the homoerotic desire within his poetry—the ultimate taboo. Straight teachers often participate in silencing practices because they are fearful of raising a controversial issue that might provoke conflict in the classroom. One young man Sears interviewed recalled a class discussion in high school: "In my sociology class we were talking about AIDS. One guy said, 'I think gay guys are just sick. How could they do that? It's wrong!' . . . Well, everyone looks over to Miss L., our teacher, for what she thinks. She says, 'I have no comment. I'm not even going to get into this discussion. I'm going to keep my opinion to myself'" (p. 391). On the other hand, Sears found that it was okay in many schools for a teacher to condemn homosexuality; the teacher would not face any criticism. Of a high school physics teacher, one interviewee recalled: "Mr. Jenson would usually drift away from the subject. He'd often bring up homosexuality. He mainly talked about the wrongs of it and how it was such a sin and that they should be condemned" (p. 390).

A final important technique of power used to keep gayness "in its place" in the school community has been sanctioning of the verbal and physical intimidation of gay teachers and students. Michelle Fine (1991), for example, reports in her ethnographic study of an urban alternative high school in New York City that a "male substitute teacher was greeted by [one of the students] as she shouted across her English classroom: 'That man's a faggot, right? Look at how he talks!'" . . . Arriving at her seat she yelled, 'Hey, Mr. Faggot, I mean Sir, you got a pencil?'" (p. 41). Fine also writes, "Dismissed as adolescent behavior, screams of 'Faggot!' echo down the hall, terrifying, stigmatizing, and isolating" (p. 42). In Sears's (1991) study, one young man remembers: "When I was changing classes I had all the books in my hands looking down and walking up. I'd hear someone mutter 'Faggot' and have my books knocked down. People were walking over me as I am trying to gather my books" (p. 240). These abuses are tolerated because gay teachers and students operate in an environment where they feel afraid to stand up for themselves, and because any discussion of gay people continues to be absent in the curriculum so that homophobia is not interrogated. All of this also takes a considerable toll. It no doubt drives many good teachers out of the profession, and it furthers the alienation of gay youth who remain in schools. For example, it is estimated that up to one-third of all adolescent suicide victims are gay, approximately one-quarter of all homeless youth in the United States are gay, and dropout and drug abuse rates among gay youth are likewise high (Gibson, 1989).

THE REPRESENTATION OF GAYNESS IN POPULAR CULTURE

Public schools have attempted to be "total institutions" in that everything students do during the school day and are exposed to in the curriculum is controllable (Goffman, 1961). Like communist states, they have been based on the presumption that if students in the school community can be kept shielded from "bad influences" and provided only "positive" representations of community life, they can be molded into "good," "well-adjusted" citizens and workers. The problem with this strategy, in the public school community as in the communist state, is that "big brother" control does not work in a world increasingly bound together by popular cultural, electronic images. A number of postmodern theorists have made the point that the public school curriculum is becoming less important and relevant to young people as they have access to a broad array of information, discourses, and cultural "texts" outside of school. We might think of this as the *popular culture curriculum*: films, videos, TV, MTV, magazines, newspapers, rock music and events, and so forth. Whereas gayness was largely or completely invisible in popular culture throughout most of the century, over the past several decades representations of lesbians and gay men have begun to surface. The effect of this is that the technologies of power and knowledge used to keep gayness invisible have become more and more ineffective and out of synch with cultural developments that are making gayness more visible and talked about. How, then, does the popular culture curriculum represent gayness and gay people, and what images of "being gay" are young people—both gay and straight—bringing with them to schools?

Rather than attempt to map out a broad overview of popular cultural representations of gayness, let me limit my comments for the most part to film representations, and more particularly several film representations of gayness to appear in the 1980s. The first of these is the film *Personal Best*, released by Warner Brothers in 1982, and the subject of a critical essay review by Elizabeth Ellsworth (1988). The movie tells the story of two women athletes, Chris and Tory, who meet at the 1976 Olympic track trials and become friends and then lovers. They live together for 3 years, but break up after their male coach places them in competition with one another for a place on the Olympic team and after Chris has an affair with a male Olympic swimmer. The two women meet again at the 1980 Olympic track trials and reaffirm their friendship through a refusal to compete with one another. Ellsworth focuses on *Personal Best*'s reception in the mainstream and feminist press, and suggests that the film was open to multiple readings by multiple audiences. She finds that the film generally was viewed in the mainstream press as providing a positive representation of lesbianism, although because the film placed lesbianism within the context of the athletic world, one traditionally and conventionally defined as a "man's world," some cultural stereotypes were not seriously challenged. Mainstream reviewers of the film also "consistently assigned the lesbian relationship the status of a simple filmic plot device for drawing out more worthy, primary themes, like competition, coming of age, and goal-seeking" (p. 112).

Yet Ellsworth suggests that *Personal Best* was viewed in some quite divergent ways—some of them transgressive or oppositional—so that the text eluded being assigned any fixed or stable meaning. Liberal feminist reviewers, for example, emphasized an intellectual deconstruction of the text's meaning, which saw positive achievements in the film, such as "the achievement of women in male-dominated fields, and the representation of women athletes as beautiful, graceful, and strong." Lesbian-feminist reviewers "resisted the narrative's heterosexist closure and imagined what would happen to the characters in a lesbian future" (p. 113). This involved a subversive rewriting of the film, a rewriting that saw the two women as really in love and committed to each other, despite the film's attempt to trivialize their commitment. Another common strategy for rewriting relied on by lesbian reviewers was to ignore large sections of narrative material that focused on heterosexual romance, making no reference to their existence or implications for the film's authorized meaning. All of this, Ellsworth says, "raises the possibility for films like *Personal Best* to 'get it right' unintentionally," that is, to provide a space for the construction of meaning that was not intended and that subverts or inflects conventional roles and dominative power relations, for readings that go "against the grain" (p. 115).

This is also the case with another representation of gayness that was influential in the 1980s, *La Cage aux Folles*. The French play by Jean Poiret was made into a highly successful movie in 1979, a sequel followed, and it went on to become a long-running Broadway play. So as a popular cultural representation of gayness, it assumed special significance in the 1980s. The movie and play tell the story of an aging transvestite, Albin, who performs "drag" in a ritzy, glitzy Paris nightclub, and his partner and business manager of 20 years, Renato. The latter's son has become engaged to a young woman whose parents are very conventionally "straight" and represent traditional, aristocratic values regarding the importance of "high moral standards" in society. The father, in fact, is the Secretary General of the "Union for Moral Order" within the government and views himself as a personal symbol of all it stands for. In order to gain the support of the young woman's parents, the son arranges a visit by them to meet his father. Renato agrees to pretend to be straight, and Albin is to play his mother. The setting for all of this is the nightclub "La Cage aux Folles," which Renato owns, and more particularly the sumptuous if somewhat flamboyant suites upstairs where Renato and Albin live.

On one level, *La Cage aux Folles* may be read as a very conventional text on gayness, constructed within the normalizing discourse of the time. Gay men are confirmed in their role as the Other—a bit silly, prone to emotional and hysterical outbursts, narcissistic, obsessed with sex and fancy clothes, and inhabiting an exotic and "decadent" life on the margins. This was the image of the gay male that Liberace so well represented for America in this period as well. As a politically conscious gay man watching this film for the first time in a crowded theater, I found myself choking in shock and anger at these outrageous representations of gay men, unable to laugh even as the mixed straight and gay audience around me kept erupting into laughter. My shock finally gave way to laughter as well, a laughter based on the recognition that the joke was not on Albin and Renato but on the "straight" or conventional world that judged them. Within the film the world of Renato and Albin is linked to a deep-rooted desire for a space in which all people are free to "be themselves" and in which diversity is not only tolerated but celebrated. In promotional material for the home video of the movie, MGM quotes a reviewer from the Los Angeles *Times* as writing that "the film makes its point: Be yourself no matter who or what you are."

This authorized message—be yourself—has begun to surface as one of the primary codes within commercial popular cultural texts, and it is a message that like so many postmodern messages and codes is open to contradictory readings. "Being yourself" celebrates individualism and the autonomy of individuals to construct their own lives according to their own values and achieve goals they set for themselves—a deep foundational value in American culture. Hardly a subversive theme, it would seem. Yet, it becomes so to the extent that we take it seriously and begin to resist the representatives of the "Union for Moral Order" in our own communities—those who seek to rid the community of "moral decay" and "perverts," cleanse the public school library shelves of "immoral" literature, and prevent us from seeing art or films that are presumed to violate "public decency" (as Robert Mapplethorpe's photographs were presumed to in several U.S. cities in the early 1990s). The problem with the message, "be yourself," is that it fails to account for the fact that the "self" is at least partially an historical, cultural, and discursive production, which set limits on, even if it does not determine, one's "possibilities of existence." This means that we need to interrogate the particular ways that gay people have learned to "be themselves" in different historical periods and the historical conditions that make possible the constructing of empowering or disempowering identities. Throughout much of this century, one dominant, socially sanctioned way of "being gay" was to be a flamboyant, emotionally unstable, feminized male; and Albin may be said to represent this historical construction of gayness, a construction that legitimated keeping gays in their place as the deviant and neurotic Other.

Another dominant message in *La Cage aux Folles* that may be read in contradictory ways has to do with celebration of life as a carnival. It is not coincidental that the play and film are set in the world of the nightclub, where transvestite "drag queens" perform to a mixed crowd of straight and gay customers, easily rubbing against one another in friendly camaraderie—a carnivalesque world of role reversals, the suspension of conventional norms, and the transgression of established borders and boundaries. It is a world of night, of desires unleashed, and of individuals who inhabit a kind of permanent carnival of the margins. The medieval European carnival, as Mikhail Bakhtin saw it, "celebrated temporary liberation from the prevailing truth and from the established order; it marked the suspension of all hierarchical rank, privileges, norms and prohibitions for a short time, and life came out of its usual, legalized and consecrated forrows [*sic*] and entered the sphere of utopian freedom" (quoted in Quantz & O'Connor, 1988, p. 101). In one sense, almost all movies are designed to provide a safe carnival experience, and viewing them in a darkened theatre on a big screen becomes part of the carnival. Within this space and time, established symbolic orders can be challenged and new ones tried out. This, indeed, has always been the subversive potential within film. Of course, we need to be careful not to overstate the transformative potential in carnival, especially the kind produced and packaged by Hollywood. As with all carnivals, when this film ends, everyone is expected to return to the "normal" or "real" world outside, the normality of which has been confirmed and affirmed by the safe experience of briefly escaping to a marginalized world. Still, we may take something with us from carnival—such as a vision of a more equitable and humane world, or a certain empathy for those who transgress the norms of "straight" culture.

In recent years, popular cultural representations of gayness have moved at least partially beyond the stereotypes embodied in *La Cage aux Folles*, much as representations of Blackness have moved beyond the stereotypes of *Amos and Andy*. Yet in both cases we may legitimately question just how much progress has been made. Black males now are often represented as either the athletic Other (all physicality with little in the way of intellect) or the criminal, drug-addicted Other (and thus as prime candidates for being shot and killed in films). Similarly, if gay men are no longer the brunt of jokes about their effeminacy, or treated as desperate and pathetic, they are more and more represented as diseased and dying Others. Even though major films such as *Philadelphia, Longtime Companion*, and *The Band Played On* "take sides" with AIDS victims, and even though it is important to focus attention on the relationship between the struggles of those with HIV and AIDS and gays and lesbians generally, the linkage between gayness and AIDS in popular culture also must be called into question. Simon Watney (1991) reminds us that AIDS is associated not only with gay males but with Blackness and with the African continent, and that "blacks and gay men remain curiously linked—the two great indispensable Others. . . . Hence the widespread tendency of Western governments to emphasize the 'threat' of HIV 'leaking' from the social constituencies affected most severely by AIDS" (p. 98). Through the representation of AIDS in popular culture, Watney argues that "Africa becomes a 'deviant' continent, just as gay men are effectively Africanized" (p. 92). Furthermore, even though the popular cultural representation of gay identity has changed somewhat in the 1990s, much remains the same. Thus, the major "gay film" of 1996 proved to be *The Bird Cage*, a Hollywood remake of *La Cage aux Folles* set in the United States and with all of the earlier film's campy stereotypes kept intact.

Because popular cultural texts work in so many contradictory ways and are open to multiple and competing readings, it is difficult to predict their precise impact on young people's evolving conceptions of self and Other. However, since silencing and invisibility are so central to the maintenance of the closeted, normalizing community, popular culture may be subversive even when it reinforces stereotypes. Furthermore, all popular cultural texts are open to multiple interpretations. Finally, some popular cultural forms that I have not discussed here, such as the television talk show, seem to potentially open up even more room to challenge normalizing conceptions of community. Richard Mohr (1994), a leading gay scholar, has recently argued that "the clearest sign that gays are winning the cultural wars is the near total collapse in the mainstream [press and popular culture] of the taboo covering the discussion of gay issues. . . . The effect of this structural change in public life cannot be overestimated. . . . With the collapse of the taboo, straight people can for the first time really listen to gay lives, change their views, and in turn express publicly their own feelings." Gay people, including gay youth, become part of the everydayness of our lives when they appear on Donahue or Oprah. Mohr even goes so far as to suggest that the New Right is contributing to this process by promoting discourse on sexuality and gayness. "For the more they talk about things gay, the more the taboo collapses" (p. 6). Merely by representing gayness and making it part of everyday discourse, TV talk shows and other forms of commercialized popular culture challenge the worst forms of oppression associated with silencing and invisibility and make it more difficult for public schools to continue their own silencing practices. At the same time, however, by failing to help students deconstruct popular cultural texts to reveal how they work to represent the Other, and by failing to engage students in critical reading and rewriting of popular cultural texts, public schools may encourage young people to read popular cultural texts in a noncritical way, merely consuming images and fitting them within pre-existing stereotypes and biases.

IDENTITY FORMATION AND "COMING OUT" AS GAY

Popular culture may represent identity, but identity also is represented in corporeal form, as individuals actively "live" their identities and make these identities visible in their everyday relations with others. Identity formation in this sense involves two interrelated processes. First, it involves identification with groups or collectivities and with the subcultures and discourses these groups have produced as part of the process of defining themselves. Second, it involves some understanding of self in relation to Others. In normalizing communities, identity typically is constructed in rigidly oppositional ways, with one pole of identity privileged and viewed as "normal" and the other pole viewed as deficient and "abnormal." "Being gay" thus involves some level of identification with a "gay community," "gay culture," and/or "gay struggle," and also some understanding of oneself as different from "straight" women or men. Within the normalizing American community, this also has tended to mean oppositional to "straight"—in lifestyle, definition of femininity and masculinity, and so on. This means that an analysis of gay identity is never to be understood as separable from an analysis of straight identity, just as an analysis of the meaning of "Blackness" in American culture necessarily involves an analysis of the historical construction of "whiteness." How, then, are young people learning to "be gay" in the 1990s? And, to what extent do gay identity and culture pose an existing or potential challenge to heterosexist constructions of gay and straight identity?

To begin to unpack these questions, we must begin with the recognition that gay culture is not all of one piece, but rather provides gay-identified individuals with alternative ways of "being gay," some of which are consistent with keeping gays in their place at the margins and others of which are more individually and collectively empowering and counterhegemonic—that is, linkable to a new democratic discourse and social movement. The most counterhegemonic way of "being gay" may be associated with the gay rights movement, although that broad movement involves more than an assertion of rights to equal protection under the law. Among other things, it involves the constitution of a whole network of support services and organizations designed to help individuals "come out" in a supportive environment and participate in the gay community, including gay counseling services, drop-in centers, support groups, athletic leagues, choruses, political organizations, and so forth. "Coming out" may be appreciated as an important cultural ritual or rite of passage in that it involves the reconstruction of self in terms of identification with a collective, historical struggle. As a process of reconstructing the self, coming out also involves adopting a new way of "being in the world" and a new way of knowing. World views that normalize the world and that define homosexual desire as "bad" or "sick" must be rejected in the process. A politicized identity is promoted within this gay community through the use of visible gay icons and symbols such as the "rainbow" flag and banner, pink triangles and gay churches, and the quilt of the "Names Project," commemorating those who died of AIDS. One of the most powerful of these symbols, featuring a pink triangle under which is written the slogan "Silence = Death," is associated with the most militant and itself marginalized group in the movement, ACT UP. The call, then, is to speak out and be seen.

For the most part the institutions that make up this gay community are not open to adolescents, so that most gay youth continue to stay unattached and even unaware of this potential community of support. This may be changing, however. There is some limited evidence that an increasing number of youth, particularly in big cities, are "coming out" as gay within their high schools, at least to close friends, a process that disrupts closeting and silencing practices essential to the maintenance of the normalizing school community. One interesting study of identity formation among gay youth that looks at the influence of this politicized gay movement and community is Gilbert Herdt and Andrew Boxer's *Children of Horizons* (1993). Horizons Social Services in Chicago began as a community-based social service agency for the gay men and lesbians of Chicago in the early 1970s; and Herdt and Boxer studied a gay youth support group sponsored by Horizons in the mid-1980s, a support group that enrolled young gay men and lesbians between the ages of 14 and 20 years old. Unlike the stereotype of the suicidal or runaway gay youth, these youth, the authors found, had strong self-concepts and generally viewed their gayness positively. Coming from middle-class homes for the most part, the young men and women aspired to have what they called a "normal life." According to the authors, "They [the support group members] not only want to be gay but expect to be accepted by society as gay and lesbian. They do not know if they can achieve such a cultural lifeway, but they are trying very hard to find out" (p. xiv). The support group was a transformative experience for the youth, in that, as the authors note,

for the first time in their lives, they begin to talk openly about sexual feelings with peers and friends of their own age who show them respect, finding others like themselves, and adult role models, whom they can admire. Their worst fears are that they are "out of their minds," full of sin and sickness, that they are doomed to dress as transvestites, molest children, hate the opposite sex, or contract AIDS. (p. xv)

Herdt and Boxer conclude that such support groups, and other support networks in the gay community, provide a needed ritualistic context for "coming out" in empowering ways.

Some young people, particularly in big cities, are beginning to bring their "out" identities to high school, affirming who they are and asserting their rights. For example, in the study by Fine (1988) that I referred to earlier of a New York City alternative high school, she points to the existence of a Gay and Lesbian Alliance (GALA) in the school started by "a small group of very sophisticated and very 'out' gay males and lesbian females." These students "quite publicly raised questions, doing the complex intellectual and political work with and for their teachers and their peers" (p. 40). Still, Fine notes that the majority of lesbian, gay, and bisexual students in the school remained closeted, ever aware of threats to their physical and psychological well-being. Given the realities of being "out" in high school, this strategic closeting of one's gay identity unfortunately continues to be a safe response, even if it comes at the cost of lying about one's life.

It is also the case that many, perhaps most, gay-identified youth are constructing a less politicized and publicly "out" identity than those who have been most influenced by the gay rights movement and community. For these youth, being gay may mean identification with a gay community that offers an exciting life on the margins, of "partying," of constructing a "buffed" and sexually marketable body, and of celebrating life in the middle of an oppressive culture. Among adults, this is a way of "being gay" closely linked to "bar culture." Gay bars were for a long time the only "free" spaces gay people had carved out within pre-Stonewall America where being gay was okay, so I do not want to be overly critical of their influence on gay identity formation. By providing a public space for people to come together and build a sense of collective identification, gay bars played a significant role in the early gay rights movement; and it is not coincidental that the beginning of the modern gay rights movement is marked by a riot at a Greenwich Village bar in 1969. As African Americans had their churches as free spaces, the gay community had its bars. Still, gay bar culture on the whole has not served as an important site for building an empowering, nonmarginalized gay identity. One major reason is that gay bar culture is grounded in the commercialization of gayness, which means that its primary motivation is to make money through the selling of a particular way of being gay that is relatively apolitical in its implications. Bar culture, although it serves important positive roles, allows gay people only a brief escape from the normalizing community, and in a space hidden from public view, so that in some ways it has helped keep gay people in their place.

A related way of being gay represented in gay culture, especially for gay men, has been that of "sexual outlaw." If, in popular culture, being straight meant being "normal," that is, affirming (if not always practicing) bourgeois, traditional, repressive, monogamous, married sexuality, then being gay meant, by definition, the opposite. Gay identity was constructed around the experience of being a sexual outsider, deviant, and (quite literally) outlaw. One dominant way to affirm one's gayness in pre-AIDS America and to some degree today has been to accentuate an unrepressed sexuality with multiple partners. While some degree of desublimation of sexuality has been consistent with the advancement of human freedom, gay identity has meant for some an obsessive desublimation, a desublimation that reached its peak in the late 1970s and early 1980s, in a pre-AIDS America. Some gay males growing up in major urban areas may even feel that getting AIDS is inevitable and part of being gay; or they may feel guilty that they have been spared when others have not and as a consequence put themselves at risk. Consequently, growing up to affirm a gay identity is not without its dangers, particularly if that gay identity continues to be organized primarily around notions of "living dangerously."

Other features of gay culture in America currently limit its potential as a site for locating gayness within the reconstruction of a democratic, multicultural community. One of these is that gay culture has tended to be organized around an upper-middle-class "yuppie" identity and lifestyle. Certainly, the great majority of gay men and lesbians are not members of the upper middle class in either income or lifestyle, although New Right representations of gayness have emphasized the supposed fact that all gay people are economically privileged. In fact, according to a recent study at the University of Maryland, gay men earn 11 to 27% less than heterosexual men in comparable jobs. Lesbians earn 5 to 14% less than heterosexual women (Boulard, 1994; Pemberton, 1994). If most lesbians and gay men in America are not economically privileged, those gay people who have been most active politically and who have had most access to the media (both mainstream and gay) generally have been middle class. The gay and lesbian movement, like the women's movement, thus has tended to be a movement led and dominated by white, middle-class people. To some extent this also may be because openly gay-identified people often find more acceptance within the college-educated middle class than the working class, where traditional gender roles are still affirmed by many—particularly working-class males—although I suspect that this is changing as more and more working-class lesbians and gays are coming out. The problem is thus one not merely of dominant elements of gay culture representing "gayness" in opposition to working-class identity, but also of elements of working-class culture failing to come to terms with homophobia, along with sexism. Similarly and in a related way, gay culture has been represented as overwhelmingly "white," and this makes it difficult for many young Black gay people to affirm both their gayness and their Blackness. This too will call for changes in the way both whites and African

Americans construct their identities vis-à-vis gayness. For in elements of African American culture (and Latino/a and Asian culture for that matter), gayness has been positioned as a "white problem" or a contaminant from European culture (West, 1993, p. 89).

Gay culture, then, like all subcultures forged within the context of oppression, has contained contradictory currents. It contains, on the one hand, elements of a radical critique of normalizing constructions of sexuality and sexual identity and it provides space for individuals to affirm both a positive sense of self and a collective identification with a cultural and political struggle. Yet currents in gay culture also have played a part in keeping gay people in their place through the promotion of forms of resistance to "being straight" that can be self-destructive (such as the "sexual outlaw" identity); and they have tended to promote a middle-class, white construction of gayness. At the present time, there are several ways in which gay identity is having an impact on the school community and disrupting or unsettling established practices. First, regardless of how young people construct a gay identity, the very existence of more-or-less "out" gay-identified youth in schools poses a threat to silencing practices. It remains to be seen how long public schools can fail to respond to the existence of "out" gay youth and gay teachers. Second, by failing to help gay youth (and all youth, for that matter) to critically reflect on the process of "becoming somebody," and by seeking to erase gayness from the curriculum and everyday school life, schools promote alienating responses among gay youth. The high levels of drug use, high dropout rates, and high suicide rates among gay youth are at least partially understandable both as manifestations of alienation and as socially sanctioned, self-destructive ways of "being gay." We need to start holding the school accountable for failing to meet the needs of these youth. Third, as gay-identified youth are beginning to surface in schools, we are seeing an increase in incidents of verbal and physical harassment or "gay-bashing" to which the schools are pressured to respond. Finally, as gay identity has surfaced in the community and gays have begun organizing to advance an empowerment agenda, and as a strong and virulent backlash movement has developed on the political right, public schools have been caught in the cross-fire and seemingly are unwilling or unable to move in any decisive direction.

PUBLIC SCHOOLS AND COMMUNITY IN THE POSTMODERN ERA

One thing we can conclude about the emerging shape of community in America is that because it is more fragmented, it is becoming more difficult to construct a "public" curriculum that has broad-based support. This represents a problem for both democratic progressive and neoconservative or New Right forces. The

New Right has not been successful in building a broad-based power bloc or articulating a "public" discourse on educational and social problems with broad appeal. However, neither have any of the new social movements on the political left. For the time being, at least, this means that the public schools are caught in a dilemma over gayness, unable to please anyone, and unable to act without inviting attack from one side or the other. The recent battle over the so-called Children of the Rainbow multicultural curriculum in New York City provides a good example. The Rainbow Curriculum was developed as part of a 1989 resolution by the New York City Board of Education requiring lessons in the appreciation of racial, ethnic, religious, and sexual diversity ("Teaching about gay life," 1992). The Gay and Lesbian Teachers Association, an increasingly visible presence in the district in the 1990s, had been instrumental in pushing for the inclusion of language on sexual orientation in the proposed curriculum, and the final report of the drafting committee was "gay friendly." For example, as part of the first-grade curriculum the report recommended that teachers "include references to lesbians and gays in all curriculum areas and . . . avoid exclusionary practices by presuming a person's sexual orientation, reinforcing stereotypes, or speaking of lesbians/gays as 'they' or 'other.'" The report included a bibliography with three books that depict children in families headed by homosexual partners: *Daddy's Roommate, Heather Has Two Mommies*, and *Gloria Goes to Gay Pride*.

Once an initial draft of the proposed curriculum was released, the controversy began almost immediately. The president of District 24 local school board in Queens declared, among other things, that the board would not "accept two people of the same sex engaged in deviant sexual practices as 'families'" ("Diversifying schools'," 1992). Ultimately, the New York City school district became embroiled in an internal battle that led to the rejection of the Rainbow Curriculum by the school board, at which point then Chancellor Fernandez threatened to override the board's rejection. In the compromise that followed, Fernandez agreed to eliminate references to "lesbian/gay families" and replaced this with "same gender couples." A statement recommending the inclusion of "references to lesbian/gay people in all curriculum areas" was eliminated. *Heather Has Two Mommies* was taken off the suggested reading list. Interestingly, other language in the curriculum also was modified to appeal to traditionalist and religious fundamentalist groups. Out came a section suggesting that teachers challenge conventional gender stereotypes by "purposely making pink or red name tags for boys and blue tags for girls," along with a section on how people with AIDS have been unfairly stigmatized ("Fernandez modifies," 1993). Major church groups also lined up against the Rainbow Curriculum, including the Bronx Hispanic Clergy Association, the Catholic Archdiocese of New York, Christian fundamentalists, and Orthodox Jews. Yet 25 Protestant and Jewish clergy formed a council to counter the attack from the right ("Liberal groups," 1993). This points to the growing battle *within* the religious community over sexuality.

It may be that the final "compromise" multicultural curriculum constructed in New York City is the best that progressive forces can hope for in the current situation. Part of the problem to begin with was that the curriculum was developed by school district staff in the central office, with relatively little input from the communities that were to "implement" the imposed plan for multicultural education. If the Rainbow Curriculum had emerged out of community-based dialogue, it would have taken much longer to construct, and it certainly would have emerged as a compromised document, but at least the community would have been involved in a necessary dialogue across difference on sexual identity, along with gender, race, ethnicity, religion, and so on. This points to the need to forge a democratic multicultural curriculum in ways that maximize public participation, provide room for divergent perspectives, and are sensitive to the concerns of all—including New Right constituencies.

At the same time, democratic progressivism must stand for something in the way of a moral or ethical vision for the reconstruction of community. Here is where I think the discourses of critical pedagogy and feminist pedagogy, as they have developed in the liberal arts academy over the past decade or so, provide an important framework for talking about multicultural education in democratic, empowering ways and for integrating the study of gay identity and gay culture within the curriculum (Giroux, 1994; Luke & Gore, 1992; McLaren, 1993–94; Weiler & Mitchell, 1992). Within these discourses, a number of interrelated concerns have been raised that are relevant to the construction of a democratic multicultural curriculum and pedagogy. Let me then identify some of these concerns and their implications for the study of gay identity. First, and at the most basic level, multicultural education is linked to the protection and extension of certain democratic "virtues," including the protection of minority rights and individual freedoms, equity, respect for difference, and (in fullest form) the development of interlocking webs of caring, supportive relations among invidividuals. This implies at the very least that educators should involve young people in a discussion of gay identity within the context of a discussion of human rights in a democratic community, and it may extend to a discussion of caring for Others, including the gay Other, in a community. Second, democratic multicultural education must challenge "essentialistic" world views that take categories such as gender, sexual identity, and race for granted as "natural" categories having fixed meaning. While our race, gender, and sexuality may, at least to a good degree, be fairly fixed or given, what we make of being gay or straight, man or woman, Black or white, and so on, is very much cultural as well as personal. Third, and related to the previous point, multicultural education is reconceptualized in terms of crossing or rupturing the borders that separate individuals into neat categories and camps. As Russell Ferguson (1990) puts it, "As we enter into language we must simultaneously negotiate the crude classifications which are imposed upon us and create our own identities out of the twisted skins of our backgrounds" (p. 13). One way to rupture the boundaries between groups is to emphasize the multiple subject positions (class, race, gender, sexuality, etc.) we all occupy. Thus, I am not merely a gay person, but rather a gay, white, male with a particular working-class background and middle-class status and occupation. As an individual, my identity is multifaceted and this means that I am freer to "make myself" as a unique subjectivity.

Fourth, a democratic multicultural education must be directed toward help-ing young people build alliances and see the interconnectedness between differ-ent arenas of identity formation and cultural struggle. This is absolutely essential if we are to rekindle a sense of community in America. I have suggested in this chapter that all marginalized groups in American culture share a common source of oppression in the ideology of the normalizing community that con-structs a cultural center and relegates Others to the margins. There are more specific cultural and historical linkages between identity struggles as well. When we examine gayness, for example, we are inevitably drawn into an examination of gender and thus "maleness" and "femaleness" as well, for the historical treatment and representation of women and gays have been very similar in this culture and may be related to a common patriarchal world view. Within this world view, "real men" are separated from all women and from gay men. This is the reason why it so important for many traditional straight men to "see" gay men as the Other, and this has been accomplished by understanding gay men as less than men, as feminized men, and as sissies. Thus, the gay and lesbian movements, with their challenge to these stereotypical constructions of gayness, are part of something much bigger than sexual identity. Straight women, because they have developed their own critique of patriarchy and be-cause they can relate to marginalization, generally have been most supportive of the gay movement. The challenge is to engage straight men in a deconstruc-tive analysis of how they understand "being straight" in ways that involve treat-ing women and gays as Others. This is a challenge since, as William Pinar (1994) observes, "men have no theoretical apparatus, no parallel to feminisim, to help them to understand what has happened and is happening to them" (p. 187). The public schools, it seems to me, have a responsibility to help young men begin to develop such a theoretical apparatus.

Finally, a democratic multicultural education must become a dialogue in which all "voices" are heard and all "truths" are understood as partial and positioned. The objective of classroom discourse thus is not so much to achieve consensus on one "true" or "objective" depiction of reality, but rather to clar-ify differences and agreements, work toward coalition building across difference when possible, and build relationships based on caring and equity. This will require learning to live with the contradictions and ambiguities of supporting democratic beliefs and values in ways that are not coercive or overbearing. We cannot and should not attempt to impose ''politically correct'' beliefs on students; but we have a responsibility as public educators in a democratic society to engage them in a dialogue in which all voices get heard or represented and in which gay students and teachers feel free to ''come out'' and find their own voices.

7

Stories of Colonial and Postcolonial Education

MODERNISM WAS, in essence, a European project—at least throughout the nineteenth and much of the twentieth centuries. It was more than European in origin, however; it also was based on a racial dualism that separated the "civilized" European from the "savage" non-European. For example, Edward Said (1978), in his historical study of the representation of Arab and Muslim peoples in British colonial-era texts, shows how these texts created an image of the Oriental Other as exotic, sensual, animalistic, deceitful, and childlike—all of which allowed the European to be positioned as "normal," rational, civilized, law-abiding, and parental. Said and other postcolonial scholars have begun to make us aware of just how much European culture and "white" racial identity have been implicated in colonial projects in the nineteenth and twentieth centuries and how much "progress" in the modern era has been tied to European cultural hegemony. According to the colonial mind-set, and the new "science" of social Darwinism, Europeans were not only more powerful, and thus able to dominate "weaker" cultures, but actually imbued with the moral obligation to help lead cultures at a "lower" developmental level into the light of reason and civilization (Bowler, 1989). While the United States never has been a colonial power in quite the same way that Great Britain and France were at the height of their world empires, to the extent that it has been a hegemonic "white" culture throughout the nineteenth and twentieth centuries, we do not have to look very far to find evidence of colonial thinking and colonial practice in the United States. Moving beyond this colonial mind-set is one of the greatest challenges we will face as a nation in the twenty-first century. For as America becomes more diverse racially, the persistence of colonial beliefs and practices threatens to undermine efforts to reconstruct American culture around multiculturalism and racial equity.

It is important not to think of colonialism as merely or exclusively a mind-set. As Said remarks, "The Orient is an integral part of European *material* civilization and culture." It has been associated with "supporting institutions, vocabulary, scholarship, imagery, doctrines, and even colonial bureaucracies and colonial styles" (p. 2). This is where education enters the picture. As an important agent of modernization, schooling proved to be an important agent of colonialism as well, designed to teach colonial subjects their place in the "great chain of being." While colonial education took on diverse and unique forms, in almost all of its forms it was associated with several defining characteristics. First, colonial education involved the imposition of a Eurocentric curriculum that effectively "erased" the culture and language of the colonized Other (McCarthy & Crichlow, 1993). Educated colonial subjects were to aspire to a European norm of cultural literacy, in which their own language and cultural heritage were viewed as a liability or deficiency to be overcome (Spring, 1994). Second, colonial education typically was aimed at assimilating the colonial subject and racial Other into the lower rungs of the colonial labor force. The ethos of colonial education thus was one of not raising expectations for students "unrealistically" high and of stressing the "natural" talents of the colonized Other for manual rather than intellectual labor (Freire, 1994). Finally, colonial education was associated with a disciplining power. Its purpose was to produce docile subjects, and this translated into a strong emphasis on the disciplining and punishment of student bodies, to use Michel Foucault's (1979) terminology. While the age of colonial education as an official institution of colonial domination is largely past, the beliefs, practices, and institutional structures with which it was associated continue to influence public education of racial and linguistic Others within Western, including U.S., culture. Because colonial domination and economic domination always went hand in hand, in contemporary American culture we are most likely to find the influence of colonial forms of education in schools serving large numbers of students who are both poor and non-European, or even more particularly non-Anglo.

It is important to remember, however, that contemporary forms of colonial education face considerable and growing opposition. For example, the civil rights movement of the 1960s may be interpreted as an incipient postcolonial challenge to the legal vestiges of colonialism in the southern states. Similarly, the struggle being waged in the United States today in support of multiculturalism and diversity is a form of postcolonial politics. We also need to bear in mind that modernism and European culture are not all of one piece, and that just as the idea of progress was used to legitimate colonialism, it also has provided a strong basis for opposing colonialism. Democratic conceptions of progress are based on the presumption that all humans are equal—at least before the law—and that they should have equal opportunities to "life, liberty, and the pursuit of happiness." Thus, within the modernist project itself, there has been some basis for a reasoned and humane resistance to the colonial mind-set. White Americans, while part of their identity has been influenced very deeply by taken-for-granted colonial beliefs, also have been influenced by this other, democratic conception of progress toward a more equitable, fair, humane, and caring society, one that is not grounded in dualisms of "us" and "them." Those white

Americans who marched with Black Americans in civil rights marches in the 1960s, who helped mobilize support against the inhumane and unjust treatment of Native Americans, who are working with diverse others in pressing local school boards to make the curriculum more multicultural, and who as teachers in inner-city schools continuously strive to set high expectations for students and affirm their cultural identities, are all engaged in postcolonial praxis.

Of course, as this resistance to colonial forms of education has increased, and as a new vision of a multicultural American culture has begun to emerge, neoconservatives are making efforts to reassert a Eurocentric, racially hege-monic culture. Recent attacks on multicultural education and affirmative action, along with calls for a return to a Eurocentric curriculum that teaches the "time-less truths," are signs of such a reactionary politics. So, too, is the promotion of supposedly meritocratic and universalistic standards for evaluating student achievement and making decisions about college admission, and the related as-sertion, made most recently by Richard Herrnstein and Charles Murray in *The Bell Curve* (1994), that individuals and groups who end up at the bottom of the socioeconomic hierarchy are genetically inferior in intelligence and that ef-forts aimed at improving their lot through education and other means are thus a waste of time and resources. Consequently, if there is reason to be hopeful that as a nation we are making progress in moving beyond the colonial mind-set, this hope must be tempered with the realization that reactionary politics that play white Americans off against racial Others continue to have a powerful appeal in the United States, particularly at times of economic dislocation such as these.

In order to more concretely locate this discussion of colonial and postcolo-nial education in the United States, I want to organize my comments around a description of two schools serving racially and ethnically marginalized students. Rather than engage in a detached, analytic description of these schools, how-ever, I want to tell "stories" based on my own experiences and observations in the schools, stories about the continuing influence of the colonial mind-set in public education and about an emergent postcolonial praxis. By indicating that I am about to engage in storytelling, I do not mean to suggest that what I have to say is fiction. Rather, I want to suggest that all research in schools and other cultural sites involves the researcher in a form of storytelling. That is, it is an attempt to make sense of something that happened or is happening, as seen from the perspective of the narrator. The process of constructing stories involves selecting certain events as memorable and locating them within a web or network of other memorable events as well as a more generalizable cultural and/or historical context. In this process images, cultural myths, and metaphors are employed to illuminate the broader relevance of the story. The purpose of storytelling, at least from a critical standpoint, is not only to help us see meaning in the concreteness of everyday life, but also to help us re-script everyday life in institutional sites consistent with democratic progressive values and visions of progress (Witherell & Noddings, 1991). Of course, if we view our research as a form of storytelling, we may be tempted to distort things to "tell a good story" in which everything fits neatly and predictably together. To prevent this, researchers as storytellers need constantly to look for ways in which what they see and experience in schools both confirms and challenges their expectations. They also should strive to make their stories as complex, multidimensional, and open to new interpretations and insights as possible. Given the inherent limitations of stories as expressive of one person's perspective, I believe there is much to be learned from this type of personal narrative, even if it challenges many traditional research methodologies.

The first story that follows describes a U.S. Bureau of Indian Affairs (BIA) boarding school on the Navajo Indian Reservation in the Southwest in the late 1960s, based on my observations and experiences living and teaching in the school for 5 weeks as part of Peace Corps training. My observations and reflections were recorded in a journal at that time; and over several decades of telling the "story" of the school in various classes I have taught at the university, it has been condensed or crystallized down into its basic elements. To me, the story is about colonial education in an almost classic form, since the BIA is the closest thing to a formally colonial institution one can find in the United States. The second story is based on my much more recent and extended work in an inner-city middle school in the midwest serving poor African American and Appalachian students. Over the course of two years (1992–1994) I spent approximately one-half day each week observing and working in the school as part of a school–university "partnership" in school renewal. Since then, I have continued to follow developments in the school through occasional visits. Both stories point to the contradictory and ambiguous quality of life in schools serving marginalized social groups. The primary story in both cases, unfortunately, is about how persistent colonial beliefs and practices are in the education of racial and ethnic others in the late twentieth century, although both stories (and particularly the latter one) provide evidence of emergent postcolonial and multicultural educational practice. They are not meant to be stories of exceptionality—of schools that are either exceptionally repressive or exceptionally progressive and empowering. Rather, they are meant to be stories about schools that, unfortunately, are all too typical and that therefore represent deep currents in American culture.

NAVAJO EDUCATION AT RISING ROCK MIDDLE SCHOOL

Upon completing college in that tumultuous year, 1968, I was accepted into the Peace Corps and assigned to become a teacher of English in Libya, North Africa. King Idris of Libya was an unswerving ally of the West in the face of a rising pan-Arabic sentiment in his country; and as part of his effort to bring

Libya into the "modern world," he had decreed that English be made the official second language and that all Libyan children begin learning English in the fifth grade. English was selected at least partially because it was the language of the major oil companies in Libya, as well as the language of the large U.S. Air Force base near Tripoli, Libya. In order to effectively implement his decree that English was to be taught to all children, the King relied heavily on Peace Corps volunteers. I was part of about 200 volunteers going to Libya that year to teach English. The Peace Corps, in this and other programs in "developing" countries, was involved in a deeply contradictory project. On the one hand, it was involved in a form of neocolonialism, which translated into support for the forces of Westernization, modernization, and economic development throughout the Third World, often aligned in this project with multinational capital. On the other hand, the Peace Corps espoused and to some extent "lived" a very postcolonial commitment to cross boundaries and borders between peoples and cultures. The latter is what attracted most volunteers. One of the results of this contradiction is that the new, young, pan-Arabic militants in Libya associated the Peace Corps with imperialism; and when King Idris was deposed several years later the Peace Corps, along with American oil companies and the U.S. air force base, was thrown out of Libya by the new pan-Arabic leader, Colonel Khadafi, for being "agents of Western imperialism." My point here is that, in spite of the best intentions of volunteers and leadership within the Peace Corps, it was under strong pressure to serve neocolonial aims and to some extent did. We volunteers certainly did not view ourselves as agents of colonialism. Quite the contrary. Yet one of the effects of our work was to participate in the Americanization of Libya, to make it easier (among other things) for oil company personnel from America not to have to learn Arabic to speak to their Arab workers.

If the Peace Corps sometimes found itself in the awkward position of aligning itself with neocolonial models of economic development in the Third World, it also found itself in the awkward position of working with neocolonial systems of education in training volunteers. Specifically, in the 1960s the Peace Corps developed a close working relationship with the BIA to assist in the training of Peace Corps volunteers on Native American reservations. In this case, I and other Peace Corps volunteers bound for Libya were placed for 5 weeks in various boarding schools on the Navajo reservation where we were to learn some basic techniques of effective teaching and "classroom management" by co-teaching with teachers in the schools. I and four other volunteers were assigned to a middle school (grades 5 through 8) in the New Mexico "badlands," tucked up against the side of a massive and (to the Navajo) sacred mesa—a school I will call Rising Rock. The nearest small trading post was 5 miles away, and the nearest town of any size was more than 50 miles away. My initial reactions to Rising Rock School were positive, primarily because it was so reassuringly familiar. I remember thinking that the school looked like many of the new sprawling, suburban schools I had seen, and the BIA had been lavish in furnishing it with all the latest instructional technology, including early "mini-cams" and video recorders. The separate dormitories for the 300–400 boys and girls enrolled in the school were clean and modern with console stereos and color televisions in the lounges (although someone had forgotten to supply records, and the televisions did not receive any stations). I wrote in my journal that first day that "this shatters my expectations. These kids hardly seem disadvantaged." Only later did I begin to view the architecture and modern design of the school more critically. Nowhere in this architectural landscape was there a sign of Navajo culture, and this erasure and invisibility, I began to realize, were not coincidental but rather central to the very purpose of the school.

The administrators and teachers were primarily "Anglo" (as they called themselves) and relatively young—most in their 20s and 30s. They all lived along two paved streets adjacent to the school, in suburban ranch-style homes: two-story homes with two-car garages for the principal and vice principal, and identical one-floor homes for teachers. The maintenance staff were all Navajo but did not reside in the school complex. Consequently, the two paved roads, with their suburban-style homes and tended, well-watered lawns, along with the school and dormitory complexes, were the only signs of human habitation in the desert landscape—an "outpost of progress" and Western culture. A number of teachers talked about doing "time" at Rising Rock, as if it were a prison sentence, and they lived for their occasional holiday excursions back into the "real world." They viewed their work in the school as a way of getting teaching experience so that they could later get a "real" teaching job elsewhere. Thus, not only were Navajo children being educated by the white Other, but it was an Other who in many cases had little significant or prolonged investment in Navajo children or culture. There were several Navajo teachers who taught bicultural education classes; but otherwise, all adult Navajos in the school served as either custodians, dormitory supervisors, cooks, or security staff.

The principal and teachers in the school often invoked an "immersion" metaphor when they described the school's mission. This metaphor was used to refer to and legitimate a number of related practices. First, the staff used immersion to refer to the "boarding school experience." This experience was overtly designed to immerse Navajo children in "American" (i.e., Western) culture, beginning in the first grade. It did this by effectively isolating Navajo children from their native culture except for vacations and weekend visits by parents and family. Boarding schools thus were not just "efficient" in a desert region where the population was widely dispersed. More important, they were efficient as apparatuses of immersion and "Americanization." Second, the immersion metaphor was used to legitimate the fact that most teachers were Anglo. The argument was that Anglo teachers could teach Navajo children "correct"

English most effectively and prepare them to enter the modern world. Thus, one of the most important student rules in the school was that English must be spoken exclusively in all "regular" classes. Third, immersion was related to exposure to Christian religiosity. The BIA invited representatives of major Christian denominations (Catholic, Episcopal, Mormon, Methodist, Baptist, etc.) to hold after-school religious classes in reservation schools, which (at the strong urging of teachers and administrators) all Navajo children "chose" to attend. Mormonism was by far the most popular of these Christian denominations among Navajo children, and the staff presumed this was partially because it taught that Christ visited America and that Native Americans are one of the lost tribes of Israel. Ironically, however, this mythical Native American past was constructed by a white man and presented to Navajo children as their own authentic past. Students were not offered the choice of attending an after-school class on Navajo religion and mythology.

A final element of immersion was exposure to a Westernized curriculum. Teachers relied heavily on early elementary school basal readers since most of the students were reading 2 to 5 years below the Anglo "norm" for their grade level. None of these basals were written specially for Navajo children—something that has been noted in other studies of BIA schools (McLaughlin, 1993). The basal readers depicted Anglo children in Anglo homes and communities. In all classes I observed, teachers placed a strong emphasis on "basic skills" and relied heavily on individualized instructional workbooks and drill sheets—this in spite of the fact that Navajo culture values cooperative more than individualized work. The curriculum also placed a strong emphasis on career education, and in many cases lessons and units interwove basic skills and career education objectives. Most classrooms had displays of supplemental materials designed to help students explore various trades—particularly in the maintenance and service industries. Students also got "on the job" training around the school. All students worked at least several hours each day as helpers assigned to maintenance crews. In this capacity they helped wash dishes and clean tables, polish floors, and wash laundry. Although this was legitimated primarily as a way of keeping youngsters busy and thus out of trouble, occasionally it was legitimated also as educational and as "good experience." There was one relatively small crack in this apparatus of immersion. Students had one or two bicultural education classes each day, taught by Navajo teachers. In these classes, students were allowed to speak mixed English and Navajo and study the myths and rituals of Navajo culture. These classes, I was told, were a relatively new idea and had been added in response to pressure from the tribal council.

For the most part, students resisted this immersion in white culture not in violent or overtly aggressive ways, but rather through a withdrawal into self and a refusal to actively participate in class—ways that were just as effective in challenging the power of the institution and of white culture to define them.

In the journal I kept of my teaching experiences in the school, I observed that "the students are well-behaved but distant and hard to reach. They appear to pay attention to the lesson, but it soon becomes obvious they haven't understood anything." Other teachers warned me that this was a "game" students tried to get away with, of pretending to not understand or being too dumb to understand. The other major form of resistance I observed among students was that many continued to respond to questions in Navajo or mixed Navajo and English, even when it was clear they knew the English words. Other students resisted in more self-destructive ways. One of the ongoing responsibilities of the staff, including teachers, was to jump in the pick-up truck and try to round up children who had run away, back to their "hogan" homes. The year before I arrived three brothers had run away together on a cold January night. They had been found huddled together in the open desert, the two on the outside dead while the one on the inside, warmed by his brothers' bodies, still alive. There were other stories I heard from teachers of children who committed suicide in the dormitories by putting their belts around their necks and hanging themselves in their closets. As a result, boys were no longer allowed to wear belts. One frail young boy at the school had stopped talking entirely to any white staff and was slowly withdrawing into a world of his own. During recess, he often was to be found sitting alone in the sand with his legs crossed, sometimes slowly rocking himself. No one seemed to know what to do with him, and so nothing was done.

In the dormitories a staff of Navajo workers struggled to care for the children; but there were far too few staff to meet the needs of so many children. As a result, the staff relied heavily on regimentation, routine, and militaristic discipline—at least in the boys' dormitory that I observed. Every school morning, the 300–400 students were marched out of their dormitories and into the school in single file, with watchful teachers and security guards continually counting student bodies and calling out names to make sure everyone was in line. At the end of the school day, the ritual was repeated in reverse. The counting and naming of bodies was one of the most oft-repeated rituals of power in the school, and behind it lay the very real problem of student resistance by running away into the desert or by eluding surveillance on the school grounds.

There also was evidence, by the late 1960s, that a more politicized resistance to this type of boarding school education was forming. It turned out that my visit to the boarding school occurred at a particularly unsettling time in relations between the BIA and Native Americans. BIA officials and school administrators were facing resistance from a small but vocal group of parents and militant Navajo groups that demanded that all boarding schools be closed and replaced with day schools that taught Navajo culture and language, controlled by the tribal council rather than the BIA. This dispute had begun to gain attention in Congress, and in 1967 Senator Robert Kennedy had visited the Navajo reservation and joined in a call for an end to boarding schools as quickly as possible. Kennedy was then a member of the U.S. Department of the Interior, which oversaw the BIA, and head of a Special Subcommittee on Indian Education, which began its work in 1967. In 1969, under the leadership of Senator Edward Kennedy, the subcommittee issued its report—a stinging indictment of a system that, according to the report, "has had disastrous effects on the education of Indian children" (quoted in Szasz, 1974, p. 149). This "change of heart" among liberal and progressive leadership in the dominant, Anglo culture was also, as I suggested above, related to a newfound militant voice among Native Americans. On the national or transtribal level, new social movements such as the American Indian Movement (AIM) began to actively resist colonial ideology and practice. Finally, resistance to colonial forms of education began to surface within BIA schools. A group of young Anglo teachers in Rising Rock School, in collaboration with the Navajo bicultural education teachers, was actively trying to teach biculturally and struggling to learn Navajo. They viewed these activities as their own small effort to take sides in the dispute over Navajo education, and as subversions of the official curriculum that they did not list on the lesson plans they turned into the principal each week.

Since I observed and worked in Rising Rock School, much has changed in Native American education, although I suspect much remains the same as well. In the early 1970s a whole series of federal laws began shifting an historic policy of attempting to destroy the language and culture of Native Americans to a policy that recognizes the rights of Native American peoples to be educated bilingually and biculturally, in day schools rather than boarding schools when feasible, and in schools operated by tribal councils (with BIA oversight). Furthermore, the number of Native American teachers in reservation schools has continued to rise (Senese, 1991). Joel Spring (1994), in his history of the education of Native American peoples, notes that it is ironic that the "federal legislation of the 1970s and 1980s . . . required many tribes to discover and resurrect languages and traditions that the federal government had already partially destroyed" (p. 91).

Still, the transition from a colonial to a postcolonial form of education is full of dilemmas and unresolved questions. If Native Americans, and other historically oppressed groups, withdraw too much into their own culture and language and define themselves primarily in terms of an idealized past, they risk further exploitation within modern and postmodern culture—at least given the continuing colonial tendencies within the dominant culture. South Africa provides a good case in point here. In the 1950s, in an effort to maintain political and cultural hegemony, the apartheid regime passed the Bantu Education Act, which required that all Native (i.e., Black) South Africans living on tribal lands were to be educated in their own tribal languages, customs, and history (Dube,

1985). In this case, the celebration of Native African tribal culture by the white government was tied to a colonial project of keeping Africans divided tribally and marginalized politically and culturally. This suggests that former colonial peoples will need to affirm their own languages and cultures at the same time that they work to become part of an emergent multicultural society, a society organized around both cultural difference and cultural hybridity rather than the hierarchical "colonizer/colonized" dualism.

LIFE IN A NONEXEMPLARY MIDDLE SCHOOL

There are some exciting things going on educationally in most big U.S. cities in the 1990s. The trouble is that while the media and professional educators have focused their gaze on the "magnet schools" and exemplary programs that are cropping up in big city school districts, they have tended to forget that most schools for inner-city young people are still very nonexemplary. One of these is a school I will call Jefferson Middle School (grades 7 and 8), located in a large midwestern city. Approximately 60% of the students in Jefferson Middle School are African American and the other 40% are Appalachian American. Over 90% of all students are AFDC welfare recipients. One-fourth of the teaching and administrative staff are Black and the rest are white, including the principal. Over the course of 2 academic years (1992–1994), I visited Jefferson Middle School regularly. My primary purpose was to support projects in educational renewal involving collaboration between the school and the university; but I also spent considerable time in the school just walking the halls, sitting in on classes (at least those that teachers made me feel welcome in), and talking to teachers and administrators to get their impression of life in the school. I also met regularly with a group of staff people who formed a leadership core in the school and who were interested in "shaking things up," as one person commented.

My initial impressions of Jefferson Middle School as a site were almost uniformly negative. Architecturally, it appeared to be modeled after an early-1950s industrial plant, complete with towering smoke stack. Throughout its four floors there were visible signs of disrepair. Metal grating covered windows on the street level. Surrounding the school was a buckling asphalt lot and behind it an area surrounded by a high wire fence for staff parking. The school was bounded on three sides by housing projects where most of the students lived. On the other side was the beginning of a "gentrification" project—condominiums for professional people, for the most part without children in public schools. At least partially in response to this nearby project in gentrification, the school district allocated some funds for a school beautification project, and the asphalt in front of the school finally was replaced with red bricks, some grass, and a few trees. From the top floor of the school, looking out the windows (as so many students did so much of the time), it was possible to survey the housing projects, and even watch drug deals going down. The halls were dark and drab except for a few posters made by teachers, such as, "I pledge to be drug free," with space for students to sign, or, "Our mission: pass the IAT [Instructional Assessment Test] and the CAT [California Achievement Test]." Rarely was children's own artwork or writing displayed in the halls.

The overwhelming ethos of the school when I began my observations was that of an institution organized to discipline and punish resistant student bodies. Security guards with walkie-talkies patrolled the halls, and between classes students were to be found hiding in the stairwells. The in-school detention room often was packed to overflowing. Students spent their time in detention copying their "student rights" over and over again—often 100 times or more. These "rights" were actually classroom rules of conduct, such as "students have the right to listen to the teacher without being disrupted by others," "students have the right to speak without being interrupted," and so forth. This disciplinary environment in the school, however, did not seem to be very effective in reducing conflict. By increasing tensions between students and staff, it may even have contributed to discipline problems.

My conversations with teachers and administrators indicated that they had a strong sense of being disempowered within the large, bureaucratic school system. They talked of being at the bottom of a long "pecking order" of middle schools in the district and often overlooked, abused, and not given their fair share of resources. For example, the school needed a number of renovations and repairs, which were promised again and again by central office officials, but typically delayed for one reason or another. According to one staff member, "It's as if we keep talking, but nobody down there [in the central office] is listening." Interestingly, this comment suggests a very close relationship between feeling powerless and feeling silenced or voiceless. This sense of powerlessness also was related to the kinds of students served by the school, suggesting a linkage between teachers' perceived sense of disempowerment and the powerlessness and neglect experienced by students. Some teachers complained that the school was a "dumping ground" for welfare kids who could not get into any "good" schools (i.e., magnet schools) and that the "powers that be" downtown did not care about the kids or the school. In fact, as magnet schools continued to cream off academically oriented and middle-class students, the city's neighborhood schools had become institutions that served poor, minority youth almost exclusively. At one staff meeting when I argued that the teachers should try to begin raising expectations for students beyond passing minimum competency tests, one elderly African American teacher responded, "Garbage in, garbage out. What can you expect from us [the teachers]?'' This led to a heated exchange as a number of other teachers, including most African American teachers present, spoke in support of raising expectations for students, including college expectations, and identified the teacher who referred to students as "garbage" as part of what was wrong in the school and had to change. However, it also was clear from the exchange that a number of teachers in the school did not respect the students and felt they were capable of little.

The new partnership with the university provided a base of support for those staff members who wanted to change things in the school and who saw racist and incompetent teachers as a large part of the problem. The shift in the school toward site-based management also led to increased support for changing the ethos of the school. The co-directors of the site-based management team (which represented teachers, administrators, support staff, students, parents, and local community groups) were a white, female home economics teacher and an African American male janitor in the school. Their first priority was staff development on multiculturalism and letting certain teachers know that they were no longer welcome in the school unless they could change their negative attitudes toward students. As a result, the staff did begin to change, and the new teachers tended to buy into the new ethos of higher expectations and respect for students in the school.

Unfortunately, efforts to raise expectations for students were not supported within the school district's new master plan for reorganization, a plan initially proposed in the early 1990s by a special commission appointed by the business community. The plan called for decentralizing power and resources in the district by breaking it up into several mini-districts. Each of the mini-districts was to have a somewhat different mission. One mini-district was designated as an "experimental" district, where new ideas and approaches to education would be tested for possible wider application in other mini-districts. Special resources were funneled toward this district, and many of its schools became magnet schools. In contrast, the mini-district in which Jefferson Middle School was located was designated for a special focus on occupational education, including "tech prep," an influential model of secondary education that emphasizes work skills, occupational exploration and specialization, and linkages between high school programs and technical and para-professional programs in local community colleges. In effect, the school district had decided that students in the mini-district's elementary and middle schools should be tracked toward occupational education. Of course, these students and their parents still had the opportunity to transfer to magnet schools, but this was not an option most could realistically consider, given the small number of slots in magnet schools and the fact that many had admission requirements.

Because of the reorganization of the high school curriculum in the mini-district around occupational education, the central office decided to discontinue the small "accelerated" program at Jefferson Middle School that was designed to be college preparatory. The superintendent's office argued that to continue the small accelerated program would not be cost-effective, and that it represented a form of ability grouping that the school district officially was opposed to. Ironically, in this case the district's commitment to an ostensibly progressive reform—"detracking" and heterogeneous ability grouping of students—turned out to be associated with a lowering of expectations for students to a common denominator of basic skills mastery. Within this context, the mission of Jefferson Middle School, at least as the central office saw it, was to make sure that students passed the necessary standardized tests and courses so that they could move to the high school on schedule and not have to be retained a year or more in eighth grade.

The principal had been told in no uncertain terms that his job was "on the line" from year to year, with rising test scores taken as a sign of his success and falling test scores a sign of his failure. This was presented by the district as a way of shifting power downward to the principal and holding each principal accountable directly. Unfortunately, one of the effects at Jefferson Middle School was an almost obsessive concern with testing, retesting, and preparing for tests. In intercom messages to students and teachers each morning, the principal hit again and again on the importance of doing well on tests. "Remember, students, you're here for only one purpose. You're not here to have a good time. You're not here to visit with your friends. You're here to pass the IAT test and do well on your CATs. That's our mission, so I want you all to give it one hundred percent, and give somebody a smile." There was something to show for all this effort. The principal pointed out, for example, that of all the middle schools in the city, Jefferson Middle School was the only one that had raised test scores consistently for 2 years in a row. However, the downside of this obsession with raising test scores also was apparent. On any given day, no more than half of the students were attending, cutting classes was a major problem, there were many fights and conflicts in classes, and a number of teachers were resorting to authoritarian tactics to maintain order. Jefferson Middle School was not a fun place to be for many teachers and students.

Through collaboration with the university, and in response to the slow change in the ethos of the school away from a punitive environment toward a more open and friendly environment, some of these conditions began to change. Nevertheless, the ritual of testing continued to be a primary and defining one in the school and interfered with the staff's ability to give up on repressive approaches to control. Interestingly, the most progressive, project-based, and student-centered approaches to instruction generally were to be found in the school's science classes. Since students were not yet being tested in science, and since the district had received a multimillion dollar grant from the National Science Foundation for staff development in constructivist approaches to science and math, teachers were actively encouraged to be creative and organize the curriculum around projects. For example, one of the science teachers coordinated a project with a group of students to document pollution in a local stream. Another science teacher organized the curriculum each spring around a science fair in which all students were expected to participate. In language arts and social studies there was much less perceived room for inquiry and project-based learning.

If inquiry and constructivist approaches to learning were visible but highly marginalized within the basic skills curriculum, the same might be said for multicultural approaches to learning and teaching. During African American and Appalachian American history months—which were officially recognized months in the school district—guest speakers usually were invited to talk to students, but no other organized effort was made to promote multiculturalism in the school. Outside of the context of a broader discourse on multiculturalism in the school, the "celebration" of African American and Appalachian American heritage is deeply contradictory and leaves important issues unexamined. For example, one year, for African American History Month, two prominent African American men who came from the neighborhood—one a television reporter for a local television station and the other a local minister—were invited to address students in the assembly room. They told similar stories of how they came from the inner city and "made it," so "you can too." While these are important messages, they tended to reinforce the notion that the only thing that was keeping students back was themselves. Furthermore, students were a passive audience for this event, and talking and scuffling by students led some teachers to take their classes back to their homerooms in the middle of a presentation. For Appalachian American History Month, a speaker from the local Appalachian council came to each class to display some Appalachian folk art and tell some folk stories from the mountains. This representation of Appalachian folk art tended to connect Appalachian identity with a rural, idealized past rather than the inner-city life students knew. Since the rural, idealized past invoked by the speaker was one in which a college education was simply unheard of and viewed as unnecessary, the presentation also may have encouraged some Appalachian-identified youth in the audience to believe that they did not need a college education either. My point here is not to criticize these presentations so much as suggest that they are incomplete and one-dimensional. Outside of the context of a broader multicultural discourse and curriculum in the school, they actually may have reinforced pre-existing beliefs and stereotypes.

While there was little organized effort in the school to integrate multicultural perspectives into the curriculum, a few teachers did make an effort on their own. One special education teacher, for example, had all four walls of her classroom covered with stories of African American and Appalachian American heritage. During the holiday season, she taught a special unit on the African American festival of Kwanzaa, and for each of the 7 days in Kwanzaa students learned about African Americans who embodied a core principle of African culture, such as community, ecology, equality, respect for elders, and cooperative economics. Finally, one teacher made an effort to link multiculturalism to issues of socioeconomic justice by emphasizing Black and white students' common interests in promoting equality of opportunity, since they all came from poor backgrounds. Looking out of his third-floor classroom window one day after class, he remarked to me: "You know, the biggest lesson is right outside this window. There are Lincoln Town Cars and BMWs driving by on their way to and from downtown; and right out in front are the broken down cars of people from the projects. It's two worlds." These teachers made a difference in their own small ways—along with a small group of parents who volunteered in the school and turned an unused classroom into a drop-in center for parents, and the local neighborhood council that continued to push for a more multicultural curriculum and higher expectations for students in the school.

Yet, after 2 years, I began to feel, like many of the teachers, pessimistic about the prospects for dramatic change at Jefferson Middle School—unless some very major shifts in power occurred in the school district and the community. Dropout and truancy rates had not changed significantly for the better over the several years of collaboration with the university in educational renewal, and understandable staff concerns with discipline and test scores continued to drive out or subordinate other, more democratic progressive concerns—such as building a multicultural community, teaching critical thinking, making students active learners, and developing more personalized forms of assessment. I began to think of Jefferson Middle School as a largely colonial institution, with some individuals and groups bravely struggling to make it a postcolonial institution. There turned out to be some "space" for postcolonial education and pedagogy at the school, primarily in individual classrooms. However, efforts to change the school ethos met with limited success. There were some visible signs of progress, but much more would be needed to "turn things around" at Jefferson Middle School. Partially this was because Jefferson Middle School was not a school in charge of its own destiny. Its place within the overall order of things had been pretty well established by the central office in collaboration with business leadership. Efforts at progressive change also were stymied by the continuing influence of a colonial mind-set among some staff members, who really did not believe students in the school were capable of much in the way of learning and who elevated concerns with discipline and punishment over concerns for empowering students by making them active learners. This is not to suggest that there has been no progress at Jefferson Middle School or that nothing much can be done to change things for the better. However, it does suggest that efforts aimed at promoting widespread and substantial democratic progressive change in inner-city schools must at some point take on some larger forces in the community and the culture.

TOWARD POSTCOLONIAL EDUCATION

The two stories I have told in this chapter—one about life in a Navajo boarding school in the late 1960s, and one about efforts at educational renewal in an inner-city middle school in the 1990s—share common themes, even if they describe very different educational sites in differing times. Among other things, they suggest that we are still living with the legacy of European colonialism and the forms of education that evolved out of colonial projects of economic, political, and cultural domination of the racial Other. However, these stories also suggest that we are entering new, postcolonial times, when colonial forms of education and identity formation are no longer so hegemonic and unquestioned and when it becomes possible to speak of the decolonized subject. Postcolonialism remains, however, an incipient discourse in public education, and its implications for redirecting democratic progressive projects in educational renewal remain undeveloped. Let me, then, conclude by speculating on what some of these implications might be, specifically with regard to three major themes embedded in postcolonial scholarship: returning the gaze, cultural hybridity, and the selective reappropriation of the modernist project.

The decolonized, or postcolonial, subject may be defined, first of all, as a subject who returns "the displacing gaze of the disciplined" upon the disciplining power, so that "the observer becomes the observed" (Bhabha, 1984, p. 126). Colonial discourse keeps the gaze of surveillance upon the colonized Other, and it maintains control of the process by which colonialism gets represented, so that, for example, colonial domination is related to "civilizing" and missionary projects. Once the colonized is able to return the gaze upon the colonizer, and to represent colonialism from the perspective of the oppressed, a very different picture of colonialism emerges. Colonialism can no longer legitimate itself as an arrangement in the best interests of those being "civilized." In the emerging postcolonial era, it thus becomes important to fight the continuation of colonial beliefs and practices in education by bringing these beliefs and practices under a critical gaze, "naming" them, and revealing their oppressive and discriminatory effects. This becomes the first step in moving beyond the legacy of colonial education.

One thing this might mean is that community and civil rights groups become more involved in organizing watchdog groups to keep a close eye on local schools

to make sure that persistent colonial beliefs and practices do not go unchal-
lenged. In particular, these watchdog groups might keep the gaze focused on
tracking, ability grouping, and other labeling practices and on disciplinary practices to see whether they reproduce racial or ethnic inequality, and then work
with local school officials, or through the courts if necessary, to address and
alleviate these problems. Teachers also need to learn how to turn a critical,
self-reflective gaze upon their own practice to make sure that they do not inad-
vertently promote colonial beliefs and practices; and this suggests that teacher
education programs devote much more attention to helping prospective teachers
learn how to engage in self-reflection on race and other markers of difference.
For example, student teachers need to deliberately ask themselves, Do I set up
dualisms in my classes in which some students get defined as "normal" and
others as "abnormal"? Do these dualisms reflect differences in racial, ethnic,
class, or gender identity? As public schools in the United States will become
even more racially and culturally diverse in the twenty-first century, and as all
indicators suggest that an overwhelming majority of their teachers will continue
to be white, it becomes ever more urgent for teachers to be able to engage in
this type of self-reflection.

But returning the gaze involves more than being critical of and resistant to
the legacies of colonialism both in the organization and operation of the school
and in one's own teaching practice. More proactively, postcolonial education
implies a particular form of multicultural education, involving a shift away from
seeing racial or cultural identities as separable and distinct categories of difference and toward seeing them as interrelated and informed by one another. The
postmodern, postcolonial subject is a hybrid subject, constructed as one culture
rubs up against another and produces something new and emergent. At a time
when some seek the security of returning to an "authentic" past and racial or
ethnic identity, the decolonized self celebrates the ongoing reconstruction of self
and culture. His or her identity is not constructed in opposition to racial and
cultural Others (as either oppressors or oppressed), but rather in the creative
and relational interplay between Same and Other. This suggests that in literature
classes, for example, students might read contemporary African, Asian, European, and American novels to explore how each informs the reading of the
others, or they might read novels written by contemporary American authors
with differing racial identifications to explore how each represents his or her
own racial identity and how this identity has been constructed in relation to
Others within the culture (McCarthy, 1993). Cultural hybridity should not be
confused with the modernist "melting pot" theory, which implied a melting
away of difference within a homogenizing American culture. Instead, hybridity
is associated with seeing differences, and with seeking to preserve the rich cultural and racial diversity of American culture in a way that allows us to learn,

adapt, and grow from the interplay of differences while simultaneously affirming common bonds of community and humanity and learning to treat each other as equals.

Hybridity is associated with yet another theme in postcolonial discourse: that of turning the colonial discourse back upon itself by appropriating the modernist language of liberty, freedom, and liberation to oppose colonial domination. In returning the gaze upon colonialism, postcolonial discourse discloses an ambivalence or contradiction that lies at the very core of colonialism and thus of modernism. Colonialism is a culture and discourse grounded in the splitting of humanity into two great, unequal camps: the "civilized" and the "savage" Other. Yet, as Homi Bhabha (1984) has observed, in this splitting, European culture "alienates its own language of liberty" and "violates the rational, enlightened claims of its enunciatory modality" (pp. 126, 132). Gayatri Spivak (1992) writes in a similar vein that "the most urgent political claims in decolonized space are tacitly recognized as coded within the legacy of imperialism: nationhood, constitutionality, citizenship, democracy, socialism, even culturalism" (p. 57). The postcolonial project thus is not one of replacing the discourse of colonialism and modernism with the discourse of the oppressed, but rather of disassociating the heritage of the European Enlightenment project from its Eurocentrism and from the legacy of imperialism and colonialism. In its fullest sense, postcolonialism represents a radical rupturing of the dualisms that have defined colonial culture and the modernist era up to this point—those of colonizer/colonized and oppressor/oppressed.

It is possible to see within postcolonial discourse and practice, I believe, a hopeful reawakening and renewal of democratic progressivism for a new century and a new global, multicultural world. Postcolonialism begins to construct a new, democratic vision of a world no longer structured by dominating and oppressive power relations, in which individuals come together across their differences to engage in the production of a democratic public life (Winant, 1990). The long struggle against apartheid in South Africa waged by the African National Congress (ANC) under the leadership of Nelson Mandela provides a good example of the emergence of such a vision (Mandela, 1994). That struggle always mixed militancy and a willingness to put one's body on the line (partially inspired by the civil rights movement in the United States in the 1960s) with a recognition that it would be a long struggle, a struggle that would require patience, perseverance, and compromise. Mandela and the ANC drew upon the same Enlightenment conception of universal human rights as had the American and French revolutions, but they always argued that the meanings of this language had to be revised and extended, to include a challenge to the oppressor/oppressed dualism in all its forms. In his inaugural address, President Mandela (1994) declared: "We pledge ourselves to liberate all our people from the continuing bondage of poverty, deprivation, suffering, gender, and other discrimination. Never, never, and never again shall it be that this beautiful land will again experience the oppression of one by another'' (pp. 620–621). We are only beginning to imagine what such a pledge might demand of us in the century ahead and, more particularly, what it will mean in public education. Its meaning, in the end, will need to be constructed within the concrete contexts of struggle over the direction of public education and public life. Nevertheless, it does begin to point a way.

References

Apple, M. (1988). Redefining equality: Authoritarian populism and the conservative restoration. *Teachers College Record, 90*, 167–184.

Apple, M. (1993). *Official knowledge: Democratic education in a conservative age.* New York: Routledge.

Aronowitz, S., & Giroux, H. (1985). *Education under siege: The conservative, liberal and radical debate over schooling.* Boston: Bergin & Garvey.

Barber, B. (1984). *Strong democracy: Participatory politics for a new age.* Berkeley: University of California Press.

Bellah, R., Madsen, R., Sullivan, W., Swidler, A., & Tipton, S. (1991). *The good society.* New York: Knopf.

Bernstein, B. (1975). *Class, codes, and control: Theoretical studies towards a sociology of knowledge.* New York: Schocken.

Bhabha, H. (1984). Of mimicry and man: The ambivalence of colonial discourse. *October, 28* (Spring), 125–133.

Blackmore, J. (1989). Educational leadership: A feminist critique and reconstruction. In J. Smyth (Ed.), *Critical perspectives in educational leadership* (pp. 93–129). New York: Falmer Press.

Boulard, G. (1994, October 4). Numbers. *Advocate,* pp. 30–31.

Bowler, P. (1989). *The invention of progress: The Victorians and the past.* Oxford, England: Basil Blackwell.

Brewer, D., Rees, D., & Argys, L. (1995). Detracking America's schools. The reform without costs? *Phi Delta Kappan, 77*, 210–215.

Bridges, D., & McLaughlin, T. (Eds.). (1994). *Education and the market place.* Washington, DC: Falmer Press.

Britzman, D. (1992). Decentering discourses in teacher education: Or, the unleashing of unpopular things. In K. Weiler & C. Mitchell (Eds.), *What schools can do: Critical pedagogy and practice* (pp. 151–176). Albany: State University of New York Press.

Bromley, H. (1989). Identity politics and critical pedagogy. *Educational Theory, 39*, 207–224.

Bruner, J. (1960). *The process of education.* Cambridge, MA: Harvard University Press.

Buber, M. (1958). *I and thou* (R. G. Smith, Trans.). New York: Scribner.

Burbules, N. (1993). *Dialogue in teaching: Theory and practice.* New York: Teachers College Press.

Burbules, N., & Rice, S. (1991). Dialogue across differences: Continuing the conversation. *Harvard Educational Review, 61*, 393–416.

139

Bush, G. (1991). *America 2000: An education strategy*. Washington, DC: U.S. Government Printing Office.

Carlson, D. (1989). Managing the urban school crisis: Recent trends in curricular reform. *Journal of Education, 171*, 89–108.

Carlson, D. (1992). *Teachers and crisis: Urban school reform and teachers' work culture*. New York: Routledge.

Carlson, D. (1993). Literacy and urban school reform: Beyond vulgar pragmatism. In C. Lankshear & P. McLaren (Eds.), *Critical literacy: Politics, praxis, and the postmodern* (pp. 217–246). Albany: State University of New York Press.

Carnegie Foundation for the Advancement of Teaching. (1986). *A nation prepared: Teachers for the twenty-first century*. New York: Carnegie Foundation for the Advancement of Teaching.

Chubb, J., & Moe, T. (1990). *Politics, markets, and America's schools*. Washington, DC: Brookings Institution.

Chubb, J., & Moe, T. (1993). America's public schools: Choice *is* a panacea. In J. Noll (Ed.), *Taking sides: Clashing views on controversial educational issues*. New York: Dushkin.

Claus, J. (1990). Opportunity or inequality in vocational education? A qualitative investigation. *Curriculum Inquiry, 20*, 7–39.

Cohen, I. (1982). *Ideology and unconsciousness: Reich, Freud, and Marx*. New York: New York University Press.

Corey, R. (1993). Gay life/queer art. In A. Kroker & M. Kroker (Eds.), *The last sex: Feminism and outlaw bodies* (pp. 121–132). New York: St. Martin's Press.

Cormack, M. (1992). *Ideology*. Ann Arbor: University of Michigan Press.

Covin, D. (1990). Afrocentricity in *O movimento Negro unificado*. *Journal of Black Studies, 21*, 126–144.

Cowan, J. (1874). *The science of a new life*. New York: Source Book.

Cremin, L. (1961). *The transformation of the school*. New York: Random House.

Cummins, J. (1992). Foreword. In S. Nieto, *Affirming diversity: The sociopolitical context of multicultural education* (pp. xvii–xix). White Plains, NY: Longman.

Curti, M. (1959). *The social ideas of American educators*. Paterson, NJ: Littlefield, Adams.

Dale, R. (1989). *The state and education policy*. Philadelphia: Open University Press.

Delamater, J. (1989). The social control of human sexuality. In K. McKinney & S. Sprecher (Eds.), *Human sexuality: The societal and interpersonal context* (pp. 30–62). Norwood, NJ: Ablex.

Delpit, L. (1995). *Other people's children: Cultural conflict in the classroom*. New York: Free Press.

Dewey, J. (1916). *Democracy and education*. New York: Free Press.

Dewey, J. (1946). *The problems of men*. New York: Philosophical Society.

Dewey, J. (1988). *Reconstruction in philosophy and essays: The middle works of John Dewey, 1899–1924* (Vol. 12) (J. Boydston, Ed.). Carbondale: Southern Illinois University Press. (Original work published 1920)

Dillon, S. (1995, May 25). Islands of change create friction. *New York Times*, pp. A1, A15.

Dillon, S., & Berger, J. (1995, May 22). New schools seeking small miracles. *New York Times*, pp. A1, B11.

Diversifying schools' golden rules. (1992, October 6). *New York Times*, pp. B1, B6.

Doll, W. (1994). *A postmodern curriculum*. New York: Teachers College Press.

D'Souza, D. (1991). *Illiberal education: The politics of race and sex on campus*. New York: Free Press.

Dube, E. (1985). The relationship between racism and education in South Africa. *Harvard Educational Review, 55*(1), 86–100.

Earth's noblest monument. (1923). *National Education Association Journal*, p. 115.

Edwards, C. (1986). *Promoting social and moral development in young children*. New York: Teachers College Press.

Elkind, D. (1974). *Children and adolescents: Interpretive essays on Jean Piaget*. New York: Oxford University Press.

Ellsworth, E. (1988). Illicit pleasures: Feminist spectators and *Personal best*. In L. Roman & L. Christian-Smith with E. Ellsworth (Eds.), *Becoming feminine: The politics of popular culture* (pp. 102–119). New York: Falmer Press.

Ellsworth, E. (1989). Why doesn't this feel empowering? Working through the repressive myths of critical pedagogy. *Harvard Educational Review, 59*(3), 297–324.

Escobar, A. (1992). Imagining a post-development era? Critical thought, development and social movements. *Social Text, 10*, 20–56.

Etzioni, A. (1993). *The spirit of community: Rights, responsibilities, and the communitarian agenda*. New York: Crown.

Ferguson, R. (1990). Introduction: Invisible center. In R. Ferguson, M. Gever, T. Trinh Minh-ha, & C. West (Eds.), *Out there: Marginalization and contemporary cultures* (pp. 9–14). Cambridge, MA: MIT Press.

Fernandez modifies parts of curriculum about gay parents. (1993, January 27). *New York Times*, pp. A1, B3.

Fine, M. (1988). Sexuality, schooling, and adolescent females: The missing discourse of desire. *Harvard Educational Review, 58*(1), 29–53.

Fine, M. (1991). *Framing dropout: Notes on the politics of an urban public high school*. Albany, NY: State University of New York Press.

Fine, M. (Ed.). (1994). *Chartering urban school reform: Reflections on public high schools in the midst of change*. New York: Teachers College Press.

Firestone, D. (1995, May 24). When teachers unite to run school. *New York Times*, pp. A1, A12.

Flax, E. (1990, March 14). Sex-education plan urging chastity sparks controversy in South Carolina. *Education Week*, p. 8.

Foucault, M. (1979). *Discipline and punish: The birth of the prison* (A. Sheridan, Trans.). New York: Vintage.

Foucault, M. (1980). *The history of sexuality: Vol. I. An introduction* (R. Hurley, Trans.). New York: Random House.

Foucault, M. (1982). The subject and power. In H. Dreyfus & P. Rabinow, *Michel Foucault: Beyond structuralism and hermeneutics* (pp. 208–226). Chicago: University of Chicago Press.

Francoeur, R. (1982). *Becoming a sexual person*. New York: Wiley.

Freire, P. (1970). *Pedagogy of the oppressed*. New York: Seabury Press.

Freire, P. (1994). *Pedagogy of hope: Reliving* Pedagogy of the oppressed. New York: Continuum.

Freud, S. (1961a). *Beyond the pleasure principle* (J. Strachey, Ed. and Trans.). New York: Norton. (Original work published 1920)

Freud, S. (1961b). *Civilization and its discontents* (J. Strachey, Ed. and Trans.). New York: Norton. (Original work published 1930)

Gallaher, A. (1988). In search of justice: The thousand-mile walkathon. *Social Education, 52*, 527–530.

Gay, G. (1983). Multiethnic education: Historical developments and future prospects. *Phi Delta Kappan, 64*, 560–563.

Gibson, P. (1989). *Gay male and lesbian youth suicide*. Washington, DC: U.S. Department of Health and Human Services, Secretary's Task Force on Youth Suicide.

Giroux, H. (1992). *Border crossings: Cultural workers and the politics of education*. New York: Routledge.

Giroux, H. (1993). *Living dangerously: Multiculturalism and the politics of difference*. New York: Peter Lang.

Giroux, H. (1994). Doing cultural studies: Youth and the challenge of pedagogy. *Harvard Educational Review, 64*(3), 278–308.

Goffman, E. (1961). *Asylums: Essays on the social situation of mental patients and other inmates*. New York: Doubleday.

Gonzalez, D. (1995, May 23). A bridge from hope to social action. *New York Times*, pp. A1, A14.

Gramsci, A. (1971). *Selections from the prison notebooks*. New York: International Publishers.

Gray, K. (1991). Vocational education in high school: A modern phoenix? *Phi Delta Kappan, 72*, 437–445.

Grubb, W. (1992). Postsecondary vocational education and the sub-baccalaureate labor market: New evidence on economic returns. *Economics of Education Review, 11*, 225–248.

Grumet, M. (1988). *Bitter milk: Women and teaching*. Amherst: University of Massachusetts Press.

Hall, S. (1988). *The hard road to renewal: Thatcherism and the crisis on the left*. London: Verso.

Hall, S. (1990). The meaning of new times. In S. Hall & M. Jacques (Eds.), *New Times: The changing face of politics in the 1990s* (pp. 116–134). New York: Verso.

Hall, S., & Jacques, M. (Eds.). (1990). *New times: The changing face of politics in the 1990s*. New York: Verso.

Hanushek, E. (1994). *Making schools work: Improving performance and controlling costs*. Washington, DC: Brookings Institution.

Henderson, H., & Raywid, M. (1994). "Small" revolution in New York City. *Journal of Negro Education, 63*, 28–45.

Herdt, G., & Boxer, A. (1993). *Children of horizons: How gay and lesbian teens are leading a new way out of the closet*. Boston: Beacon Press.

Herrnstein, R., & Murray, C. (1994). *The bell curve: Intelligence and class structure in America*. New York: Free Press.

hooks, b. (1989). *Talking back*. Boston: South End Press.

Imber, M. (1982). Toward a theory of curriculum reform: An analysis of the first campaign for sex education. *Curriculum Inquiry, 12*(4), 339–362.

Jameson, F. (1991). *Postmodernism, or the cultural logic of late capitalism*. Minneapolis: University of Minnesota Press.

Jehl, J., & Payzant, T. (1992). Philanthropy and public school reform: A view from San Diego. *Teachers College Record, 93*, 472–487.

Johnson, B. (1993). The transformation of work and educational reform policy. *American Educational Research Journal, 30*, 39–65.

Kantor, H. (1994). Managing the transition from school to work: The false promise of youth apprenticeship. *Teachers College Record, 95*, 442–461.

Kennedy, P. (1993). *Preparing for the twenty-first century*. New York: Random House.

Kielwasser, A., & Wolf, M. (1993–94). Silence, difference, and annihilation: Understanding the impact of mediated heterosexism on high school students. *High School Journal, 77*, pp. 58–79.

Kilpatrick, W. (Ed.). (1933). *The educational frontier*. New York: Century.

Kincheloe, J. (1995). *Toil and trouble: Good work, smart workers, and the integration of academic and vocational education*. New York: Peter Lang.

Kinsey, A. (1953). *Sexual behavior in the human female*. Philadelphia: Saunders.

Kinsey, A., Pomeroy, W., & Martin, C. (1948). *Sexual behavior in the human male*. Philadelphia: Saunders.

Kirkendall, L. (1940). *Sex adjustments of young men*. New York: Harper & Row.

Kohlberg, L. (1981). *The philosophy of moral development*. New York: Harper & Row.

Kohli, W. (1995). *Critical conversations in philosophy of education*. New York: Routledge.

Kozol, J. (1967). *Death at an early age: The destruction of the hearts and minds of Negro children in the Boston public schools*. Boston: Houghton Mifflin.

Kroker, A., & Kroker, M. (1993). Scenes from the last sex: Feminism and outlaw bodies. In A. Kroker & M. Kroker (Eds.), *The last sex: Feminism and outlaw bodies* (pp. 1–19). New York: St. Martin's Press.

Kuhn, T. (1970). *On the structure of scientific revolutions*. Chicago: University of Chicago Press.

Kutscher, R. (1992). Outlook 1990–2005: Major trends and issues. *Occupational Outlook Quarterly, 36*, 2–5.

Laclau, E., & Mouffe, C. (1985). *Hegemony and socialist strategy*. London: Verso.

Lazerson, M. (1991). Democracy, progressivism, and the comprehensive high school. In K. Jervis & C. Montag (Eds.), *Progressive education for the 1990s: Transforming practice* (pp. 41–50). New York: Teachers College Press.

Leck, G. (1993–94). Politics of adolescent sexual identity and queer responses. *High School Journal, 77*, 186–192.

Lehrman, N. (1970). *Masters and Johnson explained*. Chicago: Playboy.

Liberal groups are cooperating in New York school panel races. (1993, April 21). *New York Times*, pp. A1, B9.

Luke, C., & Gore, J. (Eds.). (1992). *Feminisms and critical pedagogy.* New York: Routledge.

Mandela, N. (1994). *Long walk to freedom: The autobiography of Nelson Mandela.* Boston: Little, Brown.

Mansnerus, L. (1992, November 1). Should tracking be derailed? *New York Times,* Section 4A, pp. 14–16.

Marcuse, H. (1966). *Eros and civilization: A philosophical inquiry into Freud.* Boston: Beacon Press.

Masters, W., & Johnson, V. (1966). *Human sexual response.* Boston: Little, Brown.

Masters, W., & Johnson, V. (1970). *Human sexual inadequacy.* Boston: Little, Brown.

Mayer, M. (1991). Politics in the post-fordist city. *Socialist Review, 21,* 105–124.

McCarthy, C. (1988). Marxist theories of education and the challenge of a cultural politics of non-synchrony. In L. Roman & L. Christian-Smith, with E. Ellsworth (Eds.), *Becoming feminine: The politics of popular culture* (pp. 185–204). New York: Falmer Press.

McCarthy, C. (1990). *Race and curriculum: Social inequality and the theories and politics of difference in contemporary research on schooling.* Philadelphia: Falmer Press.

McCarthy, C. (1993). After the canon: Knowledge and ideological representation in the multicultural discourse on curriculum reform. In C. McCarthy & W. Crichlow (Eds.), *Race, identity, and representation in education* (pp. 289–305). New York: Routledge.

McCarthy, C., & Crichlow, W. (Eds.). (1993). *Race, identity, and representation in education.* New York: Routledge.

McLaren, P. (1988). Schooling the postmodern body: Critical pedagogy and the politics of enfleshment. *Journal of Education, 170,* 53–83.

McLaren, P. (1992). Collisions with Otherness: Multiculturalism, the politics of difference, and the ethnographer as nomad. *American Journal of Semiotics, 9,* 121–148.

McLaren, P. (1993–94). Moral panic, schooling, and gay identity: Critical pedagogy and the politics of resistance. *High School Journal, 77,* 157–168.

McLaughlin, D. (1993). Personal narratives for school change in Navajo settings. In D. McLaughlin & W. Tierney (Eds.), *Naming silenced lives: Personal narratives and the process of educational change* (pp. 95–118). New York: Routledge.

McLaughlin, D., & Tierney, W. (Eds.). (1993). *Naming silenced lives: Personal narratives and the process of educational change.* New York: Routledge.

Melucci, A. (1989a). *Nomads of the present: Social movements and individual needs in contemporary society.* Philadelphia: Temple University Press.

Melucci, A. (1989b). Social movements and the democratization of everyday life. In J. Keane (Ed.), *Civil society and the state: New European perspectives* (pp. 245–260). London: Verso.

Metz, M. (1986). *Different by design: The context and character of three magnet schools.* New York: Routledge.

Metz, M. (1988, January). In education, magnets attract controversy. *Today's Education,* pp. 54–60.

Mohr, R. (1994, September 2). How things stand for gays in America. *Gay People's Chronicle* [Columbus, OH], *10,* p. 6.

Moore, D. (1990). Experiential education as critical discourse. In J. Kendall (Ed.), *Combining service and learning: A resource book for community and public services* (pp. 273–283). Raleigh, NC: National Society for Internships and Experiential Education.

Morrow, R. (1991). Critical theory, Gramsci and cultural studies: From structuralism to poststructuralism. In P. Wexler (Ed.), *Critical theory now* (pp. 27–69). New York: Falmer Press.

Murnane, R., & Levy, F. (1993). Why today's high-school-educated males earn less than their fathers did: The problem and an assessment of responses. *Harvard Educational Review, 63*(1), 1–19.

Nass, G., & Fisher, M. (1988). *Sexuality today*. Boston: Jones & Bartlett.

National Commission on Excellence in Education. (1983). *A nation at risk*. Washington, DC: U.S. Government Printing Office.

National Education Association, Commission on the Reorganization of Secondary Education. (1918). *Cardinal principles of secondary education* (Bureau of Education Bulletin No. 35). Washington, DC: U.S. Government Printing Office.

National Education Commission on Time and Learning. (1994). *Prisoners of time*. Washington, DC: U.S. Government Printing Office.

National Research Council. (1986). *Risking the future: Adolescent sexuality, pregnancy and child bearing*. Washington, DC: Author.

Nieto, S. (1992). *Affirming diversity: The sociopolitical context of multicultural education*. White Plains, NY: Longman.

Nietzche, F. (1954). Notes. In W. Kaufmann (Ed.), *The portable Nietzche* (p. 75). New York: Viking Press. (Original work published 1880–81)

Noddings, N. (1984). *Caring: A feminine approach to ethics and moral education*. Berkeley: University of California Press.

Noddings, N. (1992). *The challenge to care in schools: An alternative approach to education*. (New York: Teachers College Press.

Oakes, J. (1985). *Keeping track: How schools structure inequality*. New Haven: Yale University Press.

Omi, M., & Winant, H. (1986). *Racial formation in the United States: From the 1960s to the 1980s*. New York: Routledge & Kegan Paul.

Osborne, D., & Gaebler, T. (1992). *Reinventing government: How the entrepreneurial spirit is transforming the public sector*. Reading, MA: Addison-Wesley.

Page, R. (1991). *Lower-track classrooms: A curricular and cultural perspective*. New York: Teachers College Press.

Papert, S. (1993). *The children's machine: Rethinking school in the age of the computer*. New York: HarperCollins.

Parnell, D. (1992). Every student a winner: How tech prep can help students achieve career success. *Vocational Education Journal, 67*, 24–27+.

Pemberton, M. (1994, May). Study finds there is no "gay elite." *Gay People's Chronicle* [Columbus, OH], *10*, 1–2.

Peters, C. (1993, January 17). The second coming of neo-liberalism. *New York Times Magazine*, pp. 30–35.

Peters, T. (1992). *Liberation management: Necessary disorganization for the nanosecond nineties*. New York: Knopf.

Petras, J. (1978). *The social meaning of human sexuality*. Boston: Allyn & Bacon.

Piaget, J. (1970). *The science of education and the psychology of the child*. New York: Orion Press.

Pinar, W. (1994). Understanding curriculum as gender text: Notes on reproduction, resistance, and male–male relations. In W. Pinar, *Autobiography, politics, and sexuality: Essays in curriculum theory, 1972–1992* (pp. 151–182). New York: Peter Lang.

Popkewitz, T. (1991). *A political sociology of educational reform: Power/knowledge in teaching, teacher education, and research*. New York: Teachers College Press.

Pullin, D. (1994). Learning to work: The impact of curriculum and assessment standards on educational opportunity. *Harvard Educational Review, 64*(1), 31–54.

Quantz, R., & O'Connor, T. (1988). Writing critical ethnography: Dialogue, multivoicedness, and carnival in cultural texts. *Educational Theory, 38*, 95–109.

Ramirez, M., & Castaneda, A. (1974). *Cultural democracy, bicognitive development and education*. New York: Academic Press.

Reich, W. (1945). *The sexual revolution: Toward a self-governing character structure*. New York: Orgone Institute.

Reich, W. (1971). *The invasion of compulsory sex-morality*. New York: Farrar, Strauss & Giroux. (Original work published 1931)

Richmond, V. (1934). *An introduction to sex education*. New York: Farrar & Rinehart.

Robinson, P. (1976). *The modernization of sex: Havelock Ellis, Alfred Kinsey, William Masters and Virginia Johnson*. New York: Harper & Row.

Rodman, H., Lewis, S., & Griffith, S. (1984). *The sexual rights of adolescents*. New York: Columbia University Press.

Rorty, R. (1989). Education without dogma: Truth, freedom, and our universities. *Dissent, 36*(2), 198–203.

Rustin, M. (1989). The politics of post-fordism: Or, the trouble with "New Times." *New Left Review*, pp. 54–77.

Ryan, W. (1971). *Blaming the victim*. New York: Random House.

Said, E. (1978). *Orientalism*. New York: Vintage Books.

Schiele, J. (1990). Organizational theory from an Afrocentric perspective. *Journal of Black Studies, 21*, 145–161.

Schor, I. (1986). *Culture wars: School and society in the conservative restoration, 1969–1984*. Boston: Routledge & Kegan Paul.

Sears, J. (1991). *Growing up gay in the south: Race, gender, and journeys of the spirit*. New York: Haworth Press.

Secretary's Commission on Achieving Necessary Skills. (SCANS). (1991). *What work requires of schools: A SCANS report for America 2000*. Washington, DC: U.S. Department of Labor.

Sellers, S. (1991). *Language and sexual difference: Feminist writing in France*. New York: St. Martin's Press.

Senese, G. (1991). *Self-determination and the social education of Native Americans*. New York: Praeger.

Sergiovanni, T. (1992). *Moral leadership: Getting to the heart of school improvement*. San Francisco: Jossey-Bass.

Shaw, G. B. (1903). *Man and superman: A comedy and a philosophy.* London: Penguin.

Simon, R., Dippo, D., & Schenke, A. (1991). *Learning work: A critical pedagogy of work education.* Toronto: Ontario Institute for Studies in Education (OISE) Press.

Sleeter, C., & Grant, C. (1987). An analysis of multicultural education in the United States. *Harvard Educational Review, 57*(4), 421–444.

Sleeter, C., & Grant, C. (1991). Race, class, gender, and disability in current textbooks. In M. Apple & L. Christian-Smith (Eds.), *The politics of the textbook* (pp. 78–110). New York: Routledge.

Spady, W. (1992). *Outcome-based restructuring presentation.* Eagle, CO: High Success Network.

Spivak, G. (1992). French feminism revisited: Ethics and politics. In J. Butler & J. Scott (Eds.), *Feminists theorize the political* (pp. 54–85). New York: Routledge.

Spring, J. (1989). *The sorting machine revisited: National educational policy since 1945.* New York: Longman.

Spring, J. (1994). *Deculturation and the struggle for equality: A brief history of the education of dominated cultures in the United States.* New York: McGraw-Hill.

Strong, B. (1972). Ideas of the early sex education movement in America, 1890–1920. *History of Education Quarterly, 12,* 129–161.

Styer, S. (1988). Sex equity: A moral development approach. *Social Education, 52,* 173–175.

Sullivan, E. (1984). *A critical psychology: Interpretation of the personal world.* New York: Plenum Press.

Szasz, M. (1974). *Education and the American Indian: The road to self-determination since 1928.* Albuquerque: University of New Mexico Press.

Teaching about gay life is pressed by Chancellor. (1992, November 17). *New York Times,* p. B3.

Thurow, L. (1992). *Head to head.* New York: Morrow.

Tierney, W. (1993). *Communities of difference: Higher education in the twenty-first century.* Westport, CT: Bergin & Garvey.

Toulmin, S. (1990). *Cosmopolis: The hidden agenda of modernity.* Chicago: University of Chicago Press.

Touraine, A. (1988). *The return of the actor.* Minneapolis: University of Minnesota Press.

Uchitelle, L. (1990, June 18). Surplus of college graduates dims job outlook for others. *New York Times,* p. 1.

U.S. Department of Education. (1993). *Goals 2000: Building bridges from school to work.* Washington, DC: U.S. Government Printing Office.

U.S. Department of Education, National Center for Education Statistics. (1980). *Digest of education statistics, 1979.* Washington, DC: U.S. Government Printing Office.

U.S. Department of Education, National Center for Education Statistics. (1995). *Digest of education statistics, 1994.* Washington, DC: U.S. Government Printing Office.

U.S. Surgeon General and U.S. Bureau of Education. (1922). *High schools and sex education.* Washington, DC: U.S. Government Printing Office.

Walkerdine, V. (1994). Femininity as performance. In L. Stone (Ed.), *The education feminism reader* (pp. 57–72). New York: Routledge.

Waller, W. (1932). *The sociology of teaching*. New York: Wiley.

Watney, S. (1990). Missionary positions: AIDS, Africa, and race. In R. Ferguson, M. Gever, T. Trinh Minh-ha, & C. West (Eds.), *Out there: Marginalization and contemporary cultures* (pp. 89–106). Cambridge, MA: MIT Press.

Weiler, K., & Mitchell, C. (Eds.). (1992). *What schools can do: Critical pedagogy and practice*. Albany: State University of New York Press.

Weis, L. (1990). *Working class without work: High school students in a de-industrializing economy*. New York: Routledge.

Werner, L. (1986, December 10). U.S. council urges birth control to combat teen-age pregnancies. *New York Times*, p. A1.

West, C. (1990). The new cultural politics of difference. In R. Ferguson, M. Gever, T. Trinh Minh-ha, & C. West (Eds.), *Out there: Marginalization and contemporary cultures* (pp. 19–38). Cambridge, MA: MIT Press.

West, C. (1993). *Race matters*. Boston: Beacon Press.

Wexler, P. (1993). *Becoming somebody*. New York: Falmer Press.

Williams, R. (1989). Hegemony and the selective tradition. In S. De Castell, A. Luke, & C. Luke (Eds.), *Language, authority, and criticism: Readings on the school textbook* (pp. 56–60). New York: Falmer Press.

Winant, H. (1990). Postmodern racial politics in the United States: Difference and inequality. *Socialist Review, 20*, 121–147.

Witherell, C., & Noddings, N. (1991). *Stories lives tell: Narrative and dialogue in education*. New York: Teachers College Press.

Witkin, H. (1962). *Psychological differentiation*. New York: Wiley.

Young, T., & Clinchy, E. (1992). *Choice in public education*. New York: Teachers College Press.

Index

NAMES

Apple, M., 16, 61
Argys, L., 41
Aronowitz, S., 74

Bakhtin, Mikhail, 108
Barber, Benjamin, 11, 12
Bellah, Robert, 12
Berger, J., 54
Bernstein, B., 65
Bhabha, Homi, 134, 136
Blackmore, J., 75
Boulard, G., 113
Bowler, P., 119
Boxer, Andrew, 111–112
Brewer, D., 41
Bridges, D., 6
Britzman, Deborah, 75
Bromley, H., 21, 62
Bruner, Jerome, 9
Buber, M., 24
Burbules, N., 11, 99
Bush, G., 30

Carlson, D., 33, 44, 63
Castenada, A., 68
Childs, John, 15
Chubb, John, 6, 30–31
Claus, J., 47
Clinchy, Evans, 51, 52–53, 56
Cohen, I., 82, 89–90
Corey, R., 101
Cormack, Mike, 102
Covin, D., 69
Cowan, John, 82, 83
Cremin, L., 5, 8
Crichlow, W., 17, 120

Cummins, J., 64
Curti, M., 68

Dale, R., 60
Delameter, J., 80
Delpit, L., 10
Dewey, John, 11, 13, 14, 19, 41, 50, 51
Dillon, S., 54
Dippo, D., 56
Doll, W., 51
D'Souza, D., 60
Dube, E., 127

Edwards, C., 72
Elkind, David, 71
Ellsworth, Elizabeth, 28, 75, 105–106
Engels, Friedrich, 89
Escobar, A., 23, 62
Etzioni, A., 11

Ferguson, Russell, 66, 102, 117
Fine, Michelle, 57, 84, 104, 112
Firestone, D., 54
Fisher, M., 96
Flax, E., 83
Ford, Henry, 25
Foucault, Michel, x, 7, 8–9, 20, 34–37, 78, 80, 81, 97, 120
Francouer, R., 96
Freire, Paulo, 18, 74, 120
Freud, Sigmund, 81–82, 85, 88, 89, 90–91

Gaebler, Ted, 31
Gallaher, A., 72
Gay, G., 64
Gibson, P., 105
Giroux, Henry, 16, 17, 23, 74, 97, 116
Goffman, E., 105
Gonzalez, D., 54
Gore, J., 75, 116
Gramsci, Antonio, 25, 60–62, 74
Grant, C., 64, 66
Gray, Kenneth, 33, 47–48
Griffith, S., 96
Grubb, W., 50
Grumet, M., 17

Hall, G. Stanley, 68
Hall, Stuart, 16, 20, 25, 29, 60, 61
Hanushek, E., 46
Henderson, H., 54
Herdt, Gilbert, 111–112
Herrnstein, Richard, 121
hooks, b., 77

Imber, M., 82

Jacques, M., 25, 60
Jameson, Fredric, 25
Jehl, J., 52
Johnson, B., 43, 57
Johnson, Virginia, 95

Kantor, H., 49
Kennedy, Edward, 127
Kennedy, P., 32

149

SUBJECTS

About the Author

DENNIS CARLSON is an associate professor in the Department of Educational Leadership and director of the Center for Education and Cultural Studies at Miami University, in Oxford, Ohio. He has published articles in major educational journals, including *Curriculum Inquiry, Educational Policy, Educational Theory*, and *Harvard Educational Review*. His research focuses on state educational policy, curriculum reform, urban education, and culture and education. His book *Teachers and Crisis: Urban School Reform and Teachers' Work Culture* (1992) examines the impact of the basic skills reform movement on urban schools and teacher unions. It received the Critics' Choice Award in 1995 from the American Educational Studies Association.